Thrive 9 to 5®

Your Guide to Peak Performance at Work

Kristi Daniels

Red Tail Press
Belvidere, NJ 07823

Thrive 9 to 5 ® is a registered trademark of Kristi Daniels.

Cover design by Holly Jones, LookSeeCreative.com
Author photo by Armen Elliot Photography, ArmenElliot.com

Library of Congress Control Number: 2010916308
Thrive 9 to 5®: Your Guide to Peak Performance At Work / Kristi Daniels

ISBN-13: 978-0-6154-1121-7
ISBN-10: 0-6154-1121-5

This book is dedicated to my father, Rich Daniels, the most driven man on the planet. Thank you for passing down the strong internal drive to achieve anything I desire. Just do it!

Table of Contents

Foreword

In my profession as a human performance consultant, I am fortunate to have had many opportunities to work with high achievers from a variety of different fields, including corporations, the military, higher education and competitive athletics. One of the most important characteristics they hold in common is an intense intrinsic drive to pursue personal excellence, which in one form or another requires them to perform at their best under substantial pressure.

The pursuit of excellence is a journey that requires us to confront the edge of our comfort zone again and again; out on the edge is where the greatest pressure is felt. High achievers like the edge. They look for the edge. They even push the edge because that is where they are challenged to bring forth and sharpen their finest natural abilities. It also is where their greatest accomplishments and rewards await. At the same time, out on the edge is where the escalating pace and degree of difficulty can break them down.

One of the biggest obstacles to our success when we are operating on the edge is not being sufficiently aware of the sources of effective energy, as well as the sources that undermine our energy. Having the ability to intentionally summon and direct our mental and emotional vitality can make an extraordinary difference in how we perform in the most challenging and meaningful situations.

Recent psychological research studies on stress in the workplace indicate that many of us who operate in the fast-paced, rapidly changing corporate environment are looking for less worry, anxiety, anger and conflict; they are looking to escape the feeling of being overwhelmed. The organizing principle of Kristi Daniels' book is that it is possible to cultivate our capacity for health and happiness while enhancing our professional performance. To put it more simply, stress fades and performance improves with greater awareness and wise practices. This book is not about backing away from high-pressure situations. It is designed to help us teach ourselves to be more alive, awake and cognizant when it matters most.

Thrive 9 to 5® supports self-motivated, high-achievers in making lasting changes. Daniels' approach is outcome-focused and delivers short-term improvements as well as sustained long-term benefits. The information contained herein helps us to recognize and utilize our strengths and also to understand how our own pre-conditioning, perceptions, beliefs and assumptions can get in the way of our health and work-life effectiveness.

This book is the beginning of an exciting journey to become more immune to stress and turn pressure into positive personal power. It is filled with exciting, high-impact principles that can be readily executed, measured and sustained. In short, it is a guidepost to managing the most important elements of your personal and professional life.

One cautionary note: while the concepts in the book seem very straightforward and logical, the implementation of this process requires from the reader a high degree of commitment and self-motivation. It also strikes the proper balance between autonomy and discipline. Successful people do not like the feeling of being told what to do and how to do it. Daniels presents us with the tools to create our own personal vision and plan to support ourselves in making the type of life changes that we believe are necessary to attain the right mental and physical balance. For those who persevere in implementing the processes detailed in this book, dramatic rewards in both health and performance can be realized. Good luck and enjoy the journey.

James P. Brennan, Ph.D.
Author of *The Art of Becoming Ourselves*
www.drjimbrennan.com

Introduction

Work defined my life. I was a senior vice president for a global consulting firm working 10+ hour days, under stress and constant pressure, and tormented by what still needed to get done every minute of the day. I'd arrive to the office every morning, greeted by a feeling of complete overwhelm. I planned each day to the minute, just to have it hijacked by colleagues or clients, hour after hour of tiring meetings or the chance to respond to and solve someone else's emergency.

I loved it. Tight schedules. Deadlines. Bring them on. Success for me was mastering the intricate game of juggling all of the demands on my time, making sense of what needs to happen first and accomplishing "stuff." It was like putting puzzles pieces together each day in a pressure cooker with the alarm ready to sound at any minute. My daily intention was to accomplish more than the day before. I prided myself on getting more done in a workday than most of my peers. I rose fast in my career and made a great living.

I defined my existence with my rank and the quantity of tasks accomplished. I easily allowed all of life's other pleasures to suffer as mere casualties. My laser beam focus on "doing" and "succeeding" trumped my "being," specifically my health, connections to others and relationship with myself.

Stress, exhaustion, a thickening waist and bags under my eyes were decorative war wounds, expected by-products. I was an adrenaline junkie: irritability became a natural state of being. My relationships suffered. It wasn't uncommon for me to bark at colleagues, forget to return phone calls to good friends and multitask or zone out while conversing with my family. Early mornings and late nights in the office meant no time for the gym or yoga class and barely allowed for the thought of a home-packed lunch or snack. The idea was nice, but in reality — or rather my belief about my reality — there just was no time.

On a typical day, I'd absorb my first morsel of food at noon. I didn't eat breakfast because I wasn't hungry in the morning — flying in the face of all nutritional dogma and the importance of breaking

1

our fast from the night before. I just couldn't stomach it. I once hired a nutritionist who provided a prescriptive menu, which I ditched after the first meal. It seemed my stomach couldn't handle a banana and milk combination first thing in the morning. (Later I explored other nutritional theories and learned that for those of us who respond best to the ayurvedic philosophy, the fruit and dairy food combination is disastrous.) I had the right intention, but the wrong strategy.

My daily commute included a stop at the local café for a large cup of coffee with about an inch of half and half. I raced on those fumes for the next four hours. By the time I realized I needed fuel, I was shaky, irritable and ready to faint. The minute the clock struck noon, I busted out of the office to hunt for lunch. I was notoriously one of those early lunchers and could be found first in line at the local eateries. I'd often be racing down the elevators with the same colleagues, so I knew I wasn't the only one with the "Get out of my way, I didn't have breakfast and am going to drop" gaze on her face.

Once in that desperate mode for fuel, all of the food options that I knew were really bad for me looked really good. Cheese steaks and fries with a cola. A big fat sandwich with chips and a sugar tea. Or my all time favorite hot food bar item…heaping scoops of mashed potatoes drenched in gravy with a bite or two of turkey for good protein. It tasted so good going down, but by mid-afternoon I felt like crawling under my desk for a long nap. I always wound up regretting those mashed potato days.

By 3 pm, I'd shoot back out the door to the coffee shop for a frothy treat. And on the days where I couldn't find 10 minutes, I'd choose a can of cola and a bag of chips from the vending machine. The subsidized snack machine was one of the most popular perks in our office: any treat or soft drink for a mere quarter. My colleagues and I would roll our eyes at the thought of incentivizing junk food. With a 10-minute walk and $10 bill, you could trot off to the local health food store and grab a container of fresh, vibrant fruit, crisp veggies and a bag of organic nuts. But put any one of us in the heat of the moment when we demanded food under the pressure of a billable hour, we traded the more expensive walk for a few footsteps and spent a quarter for instant gratification. With a daily diet void of nutrients, I was ravished again by 5 pm.

I continued in this cycle for years. Until one day when I thought I would soar, I fell flat on my face.

When Bad Habits Destroy Your Career and the Bottom Line

It was the fall of 2006. I was part of a team in pursuit of a large contract that totaled more than $30 million. Everything was on the line and the odds were stacked against us. We were preparing for one of the biggest opportunities collectively for the company and for each of our careers.

As I was pushing myself to the edge of my performance zone, I thought I was ready to thrive. In the weeks leading up to the big event, my team was doing whatever it took to be smarter, more creative and better than the competition. We wanted to wow the prospect.

All of my energy and drive was focused on one goal: to win. But I was oblivious to my destined reality.

Picture the conference room scene the day before the presentation: the credenza littered with grease-stained pizza boxes and the garbage can overflowing with empty soda cans. Before I sat down to interact with the team — each of us with super-charged espresso drinks glued to our palms — I'd have to wipe the leftover cookie crumbs from the seat. My motto was keep going…keep driving…the minutes on the clock were ticking away. There was no time to think about my eating habits, exercise routine or sleep deprivation. The only thought that crossed my mind to enhance my performance was caffeinated IV therapy.

We march off to the pitch the next morning at 8 am. I stood up to start my presentation and halfway through…I froze…completely and could not think of the next thing to say.

After a 24-hour stint of caffeine, sugar, processed foods and high carbs and a fitful two hours sleep – my brain went on strike. I stared at the prospects and my team like a deer in the headlights hoping my synapses would start firing and lead me to the next word. They didn't.

I'm not quite sure how I exited the pain, but somehow I bumbled through the rest of the presentation. I was mortified, embarrassed and shocked. I thought I had prepared myself for a performance of a lifetime. But that was not the case.

The horror was over. As I exited the taxi and retreated back the office with my tail between my legs – the words from my boss still echo in my head, "OK! Let's put that one behind us and go tackle the day, we have new challenges awaiting us!"

"Tackle the day?" It was 10 am, but all I wanted to do was make a reverse commute and crawl back under my down comforter!

I wanted to quit that day; I thought my career was over. I told myself I wasn't cut out for this work.

But I didn't quit — out of fear, obligation and the need to pick myself back up again. I continued on in that job for another two years.

But that morning, as I slumped in my chair, headache piercing and wondering how I would muster the energy to be productive, the light bulb clicked on. My eyes opened to the critical connection between my preparation routine and the reality of my performance. Right then I decided that I was going to stop lying to myself. I had driven myself to the edge and was ready to fall off, damaging my vitality and stifling my career success. All of my "doing" was fueled by a horrible workstyle; how I was working did not provide my body and brain with the nutrition needed to function at peak efficiency. And the morning's performance proved my theory.

My mental clarity, creativity and memory suffered from a diet of sugar, caffeine and junk food mixed with stress and little sleep. I began to wonder how much more business I could have won or saved if I was operating at peak performance. Could I have been smarter, quicker, more productive and more creative? Personally, would I have felt more fulfilled and more alive? And how long could I continue like this before I made myself really sick?

* * * * * * * * * * * * * * * * * * *

This scene is all too common in today's corporate work culture — get it done and get results motorized by a sugar-, caffeine-, fat-

Introduction

and zero nutrient-laden diet. And it is not solely about food. Popular culprits are physical and emotional distresses — overwhelm, stress and anxiety — triggered by work-load, knee-jerk reactions, habitual behaviors and deep-rooted thoughts and beliefs. We don't perform at our best when our mindset leaves no room for vitality and our workstyle generates bouts of crankiness, irritability, lethargy and exhaustion.

What is it about our work environment — or what we believe about our work environment — that dampens the motivation to make good habits stick and the belief that success and health are mutually attainable? We give up our true power and can easily rattle off two dozen excuses for how hard it is to be healthy in a stressful environment. So the challenge is: How to effectively morph our work routine from one that depletes us to one that allows us to thrive?

I began a four-year journey, searching high and low for adequate answers to those questions. My burning desire drove me to learn everything I could about human potential, eating for energy, stress management, productivity and the impact on business results. I met with alternative health physicians and nutrition specialists to pinpoint the dietary and environmental culprits and shed light on their impact to my health. I wanted desperately for someone else to give me the exact prescription for my own health and vitality that would make me feel exuberant and help me thrive in my pursuit for excellence. Yet the harder I tried to incorporate external recommendations, the quicker I failed. I felt like I was paddling my boat up the mighty river without a motor. And the minute I got tired or failed to follow a "rule," back down stream I'd go.

The second light bulb clicked on. I realized that I was doing all of the work searching for answers because I didn't want to do the work that was needed: tune inward and define my "thrive routine" for myself. I didn't want to believe I had the answers, but intuitively I did. All I had to do was closely examine my habits and the beliefs and thoughts that drove them. I had to own my power to make the decision to change them. The task required peeling back the layers of unconscious living, testing and responding to expert recommendations and piecing the best actions into the "one-size-fits-me solution."

Once I put these strategies into action, I began to see amazing results in my work and life. Situations that once seemed utterly stressful and threw me out of whack were now manageable. I started taking 100 percent responsibility for my thoughts and actions and began responding to situations instead of reacting to them. Eternal optimism became my motto and I knew I could filter the external pressure for greater levels of personal and professional success. I created diet and exercise routines to fuel me and cleaned up my environments to support my new habits. I made time for me and had more energy, flexibility, focus and a motivating purpose.

I then began to share my "strategies to thrive" with others: empowering direct reports with greater optimism, teaching yoga in the office and introducing colleagues and clients to meditation and nutrition. We all began to thrive personally and professionally. Some individuals struggled with diet and nutrition just as I did. For others, the challenge was handling stress, setting boundaries or declaring a clear vision and roadmap for what they wanted in their careers and their lives.

In 2009, I turned my passion into a business, earned certification as a wellness coach and studied with masters in human performance and behavior change. Today, I work with dozens of clients – individuals and companies – to improve productivity, achieve peak performance and turn lackluster sales and apathetic attitudes into driving forces for unprecedented growth.

From my work, personal experience and research on peak performance, I concluded that one's ability to thrive in a demanding workplace is based on four elements: energy, adaptability, focus and purpose. Master these four elements in your work and life and you will strengthen the indelible link between your health and success. That is the crux of the Thrive 9 to 5® program outlined in this book. A vibrant mind and body can coexist with an über-successful career.

This book is part of the legacy that I want to leave behind. My mission is to inspire working professionals to achieve their full potential and honor their health and happiness, all while growing the business' bottom line.

Making changes to your daily habits in a pressure-cooker environment isn't always going to be a breeze, but the program is specifically designed for you to adopt a healthier *mindset* and *workstyle* in the midst of the many competing demands in the workplace. Thrive 9 to 5® will help you assess your workplace environment, tune into your own needs (diet, stress, relationships, physical or emotional), get clear on what you want and create your daily thrive routine guaranteed to deliver better health, happiness and success at work and in life. After reading this book and completing the exercises, you'll re-engage your spirit for work and life.

A few words about the book's structure and what you can expect: Part I provides the details on how the program works. You will take an inventory to generate a baseline awareness of your current mindset and habits. Part II provides the strategies to strengthen your Thrive 9 to 5® Mindset (what you believe and how you think), and Part III provides tips and techniques to improve your Thrive 9 to 5® Workstyle (how you work, your habits, behaviors and actions). In Part IV, you'll put all of the elements together to create your "thrive zone," a 90-day action plan for success.

The book includes a mix of assessments, exercises and thought-provoking questions to help you peel the layers of unconscious living and will help you get laser-focused in your pursuit for excellence. I've also included free online tools as a bonus to guide you through the journey. Turn to Chapter 1 and get into your thrive zone!

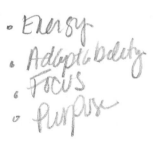

Part I

The Thrive 9 to 5® Program

1

Thrive 9 to 5®
The One-Size-Fits-You-Solution

Success is an inside game. It is not boldly prescriptive and cannot be dictated. This book is your guide to thrive in a demanding work environment, and thriving means examining what you believe, how you think and how you work. I cannot (and more importantly, do not want to) prescribe your panacea. If you do not want to do the inner work, there are hundreds of excellent health and nutrition books written by physicians, registered dieticians and nutritionists that provide detailed diets, step-by-step directives and remedies. But that is not my job, nor the purpose of this book.

I'm going beyond the surface to help you question the status quo, your mindset and your routine. What I offer are the tools and insights to change your behavior, expand your thinking, generate a greater awareness for what works and doesn't work in your routine and pinpoint the actions you need to take to operate at peak performance.

The answer to your peak performance lies in your ability to tune into what's really happening in your work and life. Your body is a miraculous system. It intuitively knows what you need to survive and thrive. The trouble starts when you stop listening to your body and unconsciously let bad habits and beliefs deteriorate your mind and deplete your energy levels. If you're polluting your body with junk food or robbing yourself of precious hours of sleep, quit expecting your body and mind to operate at peak performance!

No one knows your environment, your body, your thoughts and beliefs, what motivates you and what stops you, better than you. That's right, you have all the answers. You just need to clear the fog, pay attention, drop the excuses and put solid solutions to work for you.

Thrive 9 to 5® is your tailored system to define the actions you want to take, the foods you want to consume, the behaviors you want to adopt and the thoughts you want to think every day to drive your best work, performance and vitality. It's what you want, not what someone else says you need. But don't worry, the system will help you identify the gems you need to thrive. When you tune in and follow what works, you create higher levels of performance and success on the job.

It's time to craft your own solution to break bad habits and adopt life-lasting behavior change. Own your success, mindset and workstyle, and get into your thrive zone. It matters.

Get Into Your Thrive Zone

I'm not here to renounce workloads, hard-driving bosses or long hours in the office. What I know is that when you take care of yourself and are intentional with your mindset and workstyle, you will increase your success exponentially and achieve greater levels of happiness and fulfillment.

Imagine functioning at the top of your game — but instead of dark circles under your eyes and a haggard reflection staring back at you in the mirror, you take back your health and vitality and see a sparkle in your eye. Big results arrive effortlessly. Of course, you still work hard, but you operate in the flow where there's less resistance and struggle. Instead of constantly giving your power away and facing exhaustion, you start to own your inner power and use it effectively. You'll fuel yourself in ways that make you feel great, strengthen your resolve and diffuse stress. You will generate greater focus, increased energy and zest for your work and your life so you can work smarter, be happier, healthier and more successful.

Whether you're in an office of 3,000 or three, creating your thrive zone will help you turn your not-so-healthy, or downright toxic, work environment into a healthy haven for peak performance. Here is what you can expect from the Thrive 9 to 5® program. You will:

- **Achieve your best results at work and at home; earn more money and advance your career and find more time for life's priorities and strengthen your personal/professional relationships.** We all know that when we're effective and performing at our best, we feel unstoppable and valued. What could you achieve when you work and live at your best? A raise, promotion and better work life?

- **Own your ability to summon and direct the energy, focus, adaptability and purpose you need (when you need them) to live and work at your best.** You will improve your productivity so you can work smarter in less time with fewer distractions, relieve feelings of stress or anxiety in an instant and achieve equilibrium faster than you've ever thought possible. Create a routine that allows you to ramp it up when you have to as well as rest, recover and replenish. Your "thrive zone" will serve you in any job and in any situation throughout your lifetime.

- **Put yourself back in the driver's seat of life.** You can reverse the trap of allowing your work environment to dictate your daily habits. Elevate your standards, declare your boundaries and eliminate the need to cave to bad habits, temptations and other external pressures. Quit waiting for someone else — your boss, your spouse, your team and your company — to make your life better. Jump into the driver's seat and take the wheel.

- **Make change stick.** Rev up your internal drive and create the mindset you need to thrive. Make changes that stick by redefining what you believe, how you think and how you work. Adopt a healthy routine that endures. You'll learn how overcome resistance and change your behavior for good.

The Thrive 9 to 5® Program

The Thrive 9 to 5® approach is simple: function at your highest energy in order to achieve better results and be more fulfilled at work and in life. This book will help you develop your unique formula for success — a combination of your beliefs, thoughts and habits that aligns you with your purpose and allows you to generate the energy and enthusiasm you need to focus, adapt to change and perform at your best. It's a personal value system that can be consistently and easily repeated, revised and counted on. Think of it as your roadmap to peak performance.

As mentioned earlier, the Thrive 9 to 5® program is based on a combination of two powerful strategies — what you believe, how you think and how you work (habits, behaviors and actions).

- **Your Thrive 9 to 5® Mindset:** We enter our work environments preconditioned with a lifetime of beliefs and thoughts. Plus, we take on certain beliefs about how work life is supposed to be and then automatically adopt daily habits that fit those beliefs. The truth is: if you don't like your current situation, you can change your beliefs and your reality. The choice to change or not to change is yours.

- **Your Thrive 9 to 5® Workstyle:** Just as your lifestyle indicates how you live your life, your workstyle describes how you show up in your career: the quality of your work product, value of your skill set, the strength of your interpersonal relations and attitude. We'll examine your energy, adaptability, focus and purpose. You have the choice to define how you want to work. It's time to stop letting someone else define it for you. Raise your standards, establish better boundaries and create the success habits that allow you to declare your true essence, who you really are and who you want to be.

Chapter 1: The Thrive 9 to 5® Program

This book is your guide to snap out of unconscious living and improve your physical, mental and emotional well-being. Through this program, you will:

- **Generate awareness:** assess and identify what is effective and what is not in your mindset and workstyle.

- **Get clear on what you want**: define your vision for what you want; when you are clear, what you want will show up in your life.

- **Take action:** remove the roadblocks, clean up your environments and take consistent action towards your goals. Walk away with a 90-day thrive routine to put into action immediately.

First, you will assess your current mindset and workstyle and pinpoint the beliefs, thoughts and habits that are working for you and those that are not.

Next, you will identify what you need (beliefs, thoughts and habits) to show up and perform at your best. This includes igniting a strong internal drive that clearly defines who you are, as well as your needs and vision for your future.

You will "up level" your environments for success. That means raising your standards, setting boundaries and teaching people how to treat you. Identify the danger drains that hamper your effectiveness and replace them with energizing actions. The exercises in the book go beyond food and exercise to help you shift your mindset and rewire any unhealthy thought patterns and habits.

You'll take a hard look at your routine and identify what it means to operate in your *thrive zone*, putting structures in place to prioritize what's most important to you.

Finally, you'll pull it all together and develop your own 90-day action plan to make incremental changes and take consistent action towards your success and the life you want.

The Thrive Zone for Your Team and Company

Up until now, the journey for personal renewal — greater fulfillment in life, healthier habits, better relationships and greater self-esteem — began outside of the workplace because the workplace was one of the last environments to support a healthy lifestyle.

While Thrive 9 to 5® focuses on you, the individual, it can be adapted for teams and the entire workplace. In our workplaces today, the quest for a more efficient operation starts with an examination of organizational flow, time management and driving improvement through a structure of processes and systems. We focus on how we can better prioritize action items, manage resources efficiently and get more done in less time. Those are all great strategies to put into practice, but the "work harder" and "squeeze more out of everyone" approach leads to burnout, pure exhaustion and feelings of failure when we come up short. And how can we expect to be smarter, faster, better or stand out from our competitors in the marketplace when we're squeezing shriveled-up oranges? You can get a lot more juice out of a plump, vibrant and well-nourished fruit.

The program will guide you and your team to generate vibrant minds and bodies. Individually, you will determine what you can do to improve your health and happiness and how you can clean up your environments to support your efforts. The Thrive 9 to 5® program is the "miracle grow" for healthier, happier and more productive employees.

What makes Thrive 9 to 5® unique and differentiates it from all other corporate wellness initiatives is its direct link from an individual's health to the core competencies demanded in any workplace: energy, adaptability, focus and purpose. This book isn't about wellness for individual wellness sake alone. It's about thriving people and thriving balance sheets, a win-win combination for any organization.

It's Time. Let's Thrive!

Are you ready to break your bad habits at work — the habits that keep you deflated, exhausted and stuck in a rut? Are you ready to snap out of unconscious living and start fueling your mind and body for optimal performance, so you can be as smart, creative and focused as you want to be? Are you ready to take control of your health and happiness at work and find your one-size-fits-you solution? If you answered yes to any of these questions, it's time to make the commitment to nourish yourself and improve your surrounding environments, including the place where you spend most of your day. Uncover strategies to reconnect with your inner power. Grab a pen and notebook. Let's thrive!

2

Take Inventory:
Your Thrive 9 to 5® Mindset & Workstyle

Awareness is the catalyst for action. You cannot change what you cannot see or do not examine.

In this chapter, we will take an inventory of your mindset and workstyle. First, you need to identify the beliefs, thoughts and habits that are working and eliminate those that do not support your success. Taking inventory allows you to set a baseline to see where you are now and where you want to go, so you can measure your progress and results. It also will shed light on any repeating patterns that are not serving you.

If you think you are already aware of your current habits, delve a little deeper. Working in a fast-paced, multi-tasking and stressful environment demands the psyche to tune out and render itself unconscious for periods at a time in order to survive through the workday. And the same old routines become a comfort zone. You're reading this book to break out of the status quo, so it's necessary to wipe away the cobwebs and unearth the reasons and emotions behind your current behaviors. Resistance may creep in, but that's also part of the necessary discovery to achieve peak performance.

Now is the time to pinpoint your culprits by naming them, then swapping them out with healthier behaviors. Your motto must be: "Name it. Keep it or remove it. And thrive!"

Let's look in greater detail at the underlying drivers to your health, happiness and fulfillment at work. There are four main components to your *thrive zone*. They include:

1) **Energy:** In this section, you will identify other sources for energy as well as the triggers that drain you. Elements include your physical stamina, the enthusiasm and passion that you generate each day to get the job done, how well you maintain a results-driven attitude and to what degree you successfully engage with coworkers and achieve your professional and organizational

goals. Energy cannot be created or destroyed, only converted from one form to another. Having more energy is a direct result of your ability to fuel yourself properly, by taking care of yourself (food, drink, physical activity, rest, stress management) and having a positive mindset.

2) **Adaptability:** In this section, you will examine your flexibility and willingness to embrace change within the workday — whether it's juggling a variety of non-related tasks, anticipating and trouble-shooting problems or demonstrating resiliency to bounce back from setbacks. Adaptability and flexibility are prized traits in the workplace.

3) **Focus:** In this section, you will examine your ability to concentrate on the task at hand with urgency while keeping your eye on the ultimate objective(s). You will determine the level at which you can limit or eliminate self-imposed and external distractions, as well as improve mental clarity and acuity to allow for greater creativity, innovation and flow of ideas.

4) **Purpose:** A strong sense of who you are, what you do, where you are going and why catapults your confidence and engagement on the job, and ultimately drives your energy. In this section, we will explore your purpose, vision and goals. Purpose defines who you are, what you do and your role in your organization's success. Your vision is your ideal picture of what you want for your future. And your goals are the measurable milestones to achieve that vision. Defining all three will fuel desire and motivation for a healthier, happier and more fulfilling life.

The circle on the next page is a visual depiction of all four elements. On page 24, the circle is repeated so you can plot where you currently stand in light of these four components. Are you balanced? Is one area stronger than the others?

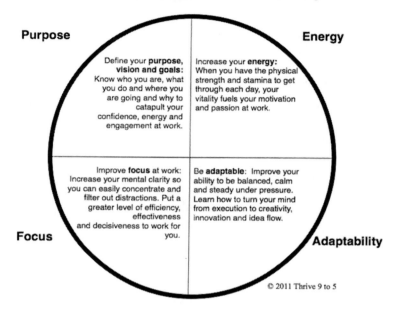

Your Thrive Zone: Mindset & Workstyle

Purpose

Define your **purpose, vision and goals:** Know who you are, what you do and where you are going and why to catapult your confidence, energy and engagement at work.

Energy

Increase your **energy:** When you have the physical strength and stamina to get through each day, your vitality fuels your motivation and passion at work.

Improve **focus** at work: Increase your mental clarity so you can easily concentrate and filter out distractions. Put a greater level of efficiency, effectiveness and decisiveness to work for you.

Be **adaptable:** Improve your ability to be balanced, calm and steady under pressure. Learn how to turn your mind from execution to creativity, innovation and idea flow.

Focus

Adaptability

© 2011 Thrive 9 to 5

Improving Your Thrive 9 to 5® Mindset & Workstyle

Looking at the four elements: Energy, Adaptability, Focus and Purpose, let's define which aspects are pulling you towards success and optimal performance, and which are holding you back. In the assessment below, you will be rating your mindset and workstyle according to the four elements. Read each statement and rate its applicability to your current work environment.

For each statement that is **<u>not</u>** true for you, give yourself a 0.
For each statement that is **<u>sometimes true for you</u>**, give yourself a 1.
For each statement that is **<u>always true</u>** for you, give yourself a 2.

Energy

1. ___1___ I'm passionate about my job and the majority of the time I arrive at work enthusiastic to tackle the assignments and challenges of the day.
2. ___2___ I put forth the extra effort to make sure tasks are completed and thoroughly reviewed to the best of my ability.
3. ___2___ I fuel myself with a healthy breakfast and/or mid-morning snacks to generate enough energy to get through the morning.
4. ___0___ I fuel myself with healthy lunches and mid-afternoon snacks that generate enough energy to get through the day. I rarely feel exhausted in the afternoon.
5. ___0___ I have plenty of energy at the end of the week and can go about my weekend routine without feeling overly tired.
6. ___0___ I don't over-rely on caffeine, sugar or other stimulants to get me through the day.
7. ___0___ I am in tune with my peak energy cycle during the day and align the bulk of my work during that time.
8. ___0___ I know how much exercise I need to feel my best.
9. ___0___ I regularly get that amount of exercise during the week.
10. ___2___ I know the amount of sleep I need to be at my best.
11. ___1___ I regularly get that amount of sleep each week.
12. ___1___ I know how to ease my stress, and do not turn to food or alcohol to take the edge off.

Energy: Total Number of Points _____9_____

* * * * * * * * * * *

Adaptability

1. ___0___ I feel that I'm in control of my life. I am not harried by life and made hostile by its demands.
2. ___2___ I'm flexible and can easily adapt to change; I realize that change is constant.
3. ___2___ I know that I don't know everything; there's always more to learn.
4. ___1___ I have the ability to exude grace under pressure; I'm calm, cool and collected in stressful situations.
5. ___1___ I regularly seek and consider alternate opinions, solutions and ideas.
6. ___1___ I'm coachable and accept constructive feedback to help me perform better.
7. ___0___ I have a daily meditation practice or routine to ease stress and keep me open and allowing.
8. ___1___ I am creative and innovative; ideas and solutions flow easily and often.
9. ___2___ I bounce back easily from set backs; I'm resilient.
10. ___2___ I wear many hats at work and can easily transition from one to the other.
11. ___2___ I know my stress triggers; the situations, interactions or emotions that create a reaction of stress or anxiety.
12. ___1___ When I feel off kilter, I know how to get myself back into balance and feeling stable.

Adaptability: Total Number of Points ____15____

* * * * * * * * * *

Focus

1. ___ I am efficient and effective and manage my time wisely.
2. ___ I rarely feel scattered or unfocused.
3. ___ When I start an important task, I can easily limit distractions in order to complete it. I am well aware of my biggest distractions and easily filter them out during the workday. I don't let technology (incessantly checking e-mail or voicemail) disrupt my concentration and workflow.
4. ___ I know how much time I can stay focused on a task and successfully block out that time when I need to.
5. ___ I give myself enough time to complete tasks and projects. I am rarely rushed.
6. ___ I'm so absorbed in my work that I often lose sense of time.
7. ___ I avoid excess sugar and junk food that limit my ability to focus or think straight.
8. ___ I am always persistent; I regularly finish the task at hand and meet my objectives.
9. ___ My physical environment is clutter-free.
10. ___ I approach my work with intensity and determination.
11. ___ I start and end my day with a clear head.
12. ___ I rarely feel overwhelmed or anxious with my task load, because I adequately manage my time and ask for help when I need it.

Focus: Total Number of Points ____12____

* * * * * * * * * * * *

Purpose

1. __1__ I know my organization's mission and vision and the goals for the year.
2. __1__ I know my purpose — specifically, the role I play in achieving the organization's mission and goals.
3. __2__ I take ownership and responsibility for my role, including all of my projects and actions at work.
4. __1__ I feel connected to the larger organization, something larger than myself.
5. __2__ I'm confident that I can deliver results; I have the proper skill-set and training for the job in front of me.
6. __2__ I understand how my work fits into a bigger goal; everything I do has an objective.
7. __2__ I know what is expected of me. When I'm not sure what is expected of me, I ask questions and/or speak up to clarify.
8. __0__ I'm confident in my career path because I have a clear vision of where I want to go.
9. __0__ I have a clear plan to achieve my vision, including measurable goals. I am making progress towards achieving them.
10. __1__ I discuss my career vision, goals and plan with my manager at least once a year.
11. __0__ My personal values align with the values of my employer.
12. __1__ I arrive at work each day knowing that my work is valued and I am appreciated.

Purpose: Total Number of Points ____13____

* * * * * * * * * * *

Rate Your Thrive 9 to 5® Mindset & Workstyle

Tally your points in each section and copy them to the chart below. Add up your total points. Give yourself 4 points for taking the test. Total Points Possible = 100.

Category	Total Points
Energy	9
Adaptability	15
Focus	12
Purpose	13
Give yourself 4 points for taking test	4
Total Points (100 max)	43

The goal of this assessment is not to give you a score of "excellent, good, fair or poor," but to support you in raising awareness for the beliefs, thoughts and habits which might not be serving you and which maybe creating a source of stress or struggle for you on the job. Once you have completed the inventory, look closely at the repeating patterns and begin to consider which elements are your strengths and which you need to work on.

Area(s) I want to work on:_____

Notes and thoughts that came up while taking inventory:

_____
_____
_____
_____
_____
_____

Below are two more circles. The circle on the left is for you to mark your score, so beyond numbers, you can see how balanced or unbalanced you are in terms of the big picture. The circle on the right is an example of what a score of energy (5), adaptability (20), focus (10) and purpose (18) looks like.

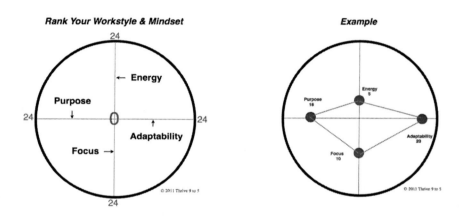

Take your scores for energy, adaptability, focus and purpose. In the circle on the left, mark a dot on each line indicating your score for that category. Mark the dot towards the center of the circle for a score closer to zero; and the dot closer to the outer edge of the circle for a score closer to 24. When you have placed a dot on each line, connect the dots. You now have a clear visual of any imbalances and a starting point(s) for improvement. A full circle indicates balance in all four areas.

Energy *9*

If you scored 18–24: Congratulations, you're thriving! Consistently generating high levels of energy takes a keen awareness of your routine and a commitment to stick to good habits. Read on to pick up more tips on maintaining your success and boosting your energy even more. Chapters 5 and 6 focus on finding your energizers and eliminating the drains.

If you scored 9–17: You may be struggling to generate just enough energy to get by. This book will help you generate a greater awareness for the unconscious beliefs, thoughts and habits that could be draining you and help you limit their impact on your day. You'll also gain a greater sense of what you need to think and do to keep your energy levels thriving throughout the workday. Chapters 5 and 6 focus on finding your energizers and eliminating the drains.

If you scored 0–8: Your energy levels need a boost! Rest assured you are on the right path. The first step is awareness — so read on to get clear on which beliefs, thoughts and habits may be robbing you of precious energy throughout the workday. You'll also gain a greater sense of what you need to think and do to keep your energy levels thriving throughout the workday. You'll be returning home to your family in the evening with more energy and smile on your face in no time. Chapters 5 and 6 focus on finding your energizers and eliminating the drains.

Adaptability 15

If you scored 18–24: Congratulations, you can easily wear many hats on the job and toggle from skill to skill and task to task. This book will help you maintain a firm resolve, yet be even more pliable and valuable to your organization, while keeping a calm, cool head. Learn how to become more adaptable and flexible in Chapters 7 and 8.

If you scored 9–17: You understand what it takes to be flexible, even if you don't exhibit the quality at all times. This book will help you embrace change and be even more pliable and valuable to your organization, while keeping a calm, cool head. Learn how to become more adaptable and flexible in Chapters 7 and 8.

If you scored 0–8: You may be experiencing high levels of stress and anxiety and at times feel out of control. This book will guide you back into the driver's seat at work, so you will decrease the charge of your usual triggers and be able to demonstrate flexibility with ease and grace. Learn how to become more adaptable and flexible in Chapters 7 and 8.

Focus

If you scored 18–24: Congratulations, you're a well-focused machine! You've got a keen sense of how to limit distractions so you can be absorbed in your work and get things done. Read on for more tips on how to structure your environment for maximum focus and concentration. Chapter 9 discusses how to hone your focus in greater detail.

If you scored 9–17: You know what it takes to focus, but your ability to concentrate may be erratic. This book will help you reach new levels of intensity and concentration. Chapter 9 discusses how to hone your focus in greater detail.

If you scored 0–8: You may have too many distractions taking you off track during the day. Never fear, you will learn how to limit distractions and create an environment conducive to concentration and focus. Chapter 9 discusses how to hone your focus in greater detail.

Purpose | 3

If you scored 18–24: Congratulations, you are in tune with your purpose and mission, and understand how your work supports your organization's core goals. With this strong foundation, you easily prioritize and execute tasks, measure effectiveness and know that you are valued. This strong sense of purpose builds your confidence and engagement on the job. Turn to Chapters 10 and 11 to see how you can build on your strong foundation and set a clearer vision and goals for even more effectiveness on the job.

If you scored 9–17: You may not be 100 percent sure of your purpose or understand how your work supports your organization's core goals. It's time to get clear and identify what you want out of your work and life. Chapter 10 will help you get clarity through a series of exercises designed to help you define your purpose. Chapter 11 will guide you to create a compelling vision and goals for your future.

If you scored 0–8: You are unclear about your purpose and may not see how your work supports the organization's core goals. Chapters 10 and 11 will be vital to helping you achieve clarity on your purpose, vision and goals.

The chapters that follow will examine each of these four elements, offering the opportunity for greater awareness and strategies to improve your health, happiness and performance.

Part II

The Thrive 9 to 5® Mindset

3

Your Thrive 9 to 5® Mindset:
Change Your Beliefs and Thoughts to Change Your Habits

"Our beliefs about ourselves and the nature of our abilities...determine how we interpret our experiences and can set the boundaries on what we accomplish." — *Daniel Pink, author of Drive, summarizing insights on motivation by Carol Dweck, professor of psychology at Stanford University[1]*

The quest for peak performance and achieving professional goals focuses on doing and taking action. Our actions produce our results, and the more effective our actions, the better the results. This is undeniably true, but there's another critical link in the equation that is often overlooked in the business world: our beliefs and thoughts drive our actions.

Changing your beliefs, thoughts and habits to be healthier, happier and more fulfilled on the job is a choice. According to psychiatrist William Glasser, "all we do is behave," and our "total behavior"[2] is made up of four components — two in which we have considerable control or choice over (acting and thinking) and two in which we have little ability to control or choose (feeling and physiology). Glasser suggests the four components of behavior are closely intertwined and therefore, the choices we make in our thinking and acting greatly affect our feeling and physiology. And conversely, we can only control our feeling and physiology indirectly through how we choose to act and think. So ignite a thrive mindset and choose the best thoughts and actions, and you will achieve a greater level of success and feel great about it!

In this section (Part II), we will focus on your Thrive 9 to 5® Mindset (your beliefs and thoughts.) In this chapter, you will discover the elements behind your internal drive and how to align your beliefs and thoughts with the results you desire at work and in life. In Part III, we will focus on your Thrive 9 to 5® workstyle, specifically your habits that make up your daily routine.

Your Thrive 9 to 5® Mindset becomes a framework for thinking that empowers you to generate a strong internal drive for greater motivation and productivity. The stronger your internal drive, the better you can manage all of the external influences that might be pulling you off track. Think of it as the internal spark for your engine — the one that keeps you moving, driving forward, open to possibilities and strong enough to withstand pressures from people and your environment, as well as self-imposed blocks.

Some people are gifted with a strong internal drive and can set a goal, move forward with laser focus, and work hard to see it through to completion. No fanfare, no drama, just hard-core grit and persistence. If you fall into that category, kudos and thrive on!

For the rest of us, the journey isn't always that simple. We might set out with good intentions, but become stuck, get sidetracked or procrastinate and never wind up moving into action or achieving the goal. And the road can be miserable, quite simply because we make it miserable. If you've ever set a New Year's resolution that fell off your priority list by February and you beat yourself up every day until the following New Year's when you started again, you know what I'm talking about.

False Beliefs, Negative Thoughts and Destructive Self-Talk Stall Your Drive

"How we see things effects how much energy we have for doing things and our choices about where to channel the energy we have." — Jon Kabat-Zinn, Ph.D, Professor of Medicine Emeritus and founding director of the Stress Reduction Clinic and the Center for Mindfulness in Medicine, Health Care, and Society at the University of Massachusetts Medical School

False beliefs, negative thoughts and destructive self-talk can act as barriers to success and limit the valuable energy you need to reach your potential. And let's face it, untruths, negativity and destructive words are everywhere.

Psychologists tell us we think 50,000 thoughts a day — between 1,000 and 5,000 thoughts in a single hour. Many of those thoughts are about ourselves and about our performance — our worthiness, our capability and our significance. Your thoughts are measurable units of energy — biochemical impulses — and have the power to generate a physiological change in your body. Simply put, the thoughts you hear from others or think or repeat to yourself every minute of every day impact the quality of your health, peace of mind and success.

We are bombarded with external messages every minute of our waking lives in the form of the news, magazines, friends, family and colleagues. "Eat this food, drink this, not that...try this diet, this fitness routine...try harder. If you don't succeed, there's something wrong with you. The economy is tanking. Unemployment is at its highest...etc." The constant whirlwind of information can create an immediate reaction of stress and uncertainty. Over the long term, it can brainwash our minds so we think less of ourselves, doubt our intuitive ability to know what's right for us and question our ability to succeed. Comparison always creates a dangerous trap. You hear what others think or you see what they do and you immediately line yourself up next to them. If your negative self-talk is already a cacophony, you'll always emerge less than, which only adds to and confirms the same old tune.

Sometimes the destructive self-talk may not come as a voice in your head, but a feeling in your gut. Working through the inventory in Chapter 2, you may have come up against some resistance disguised as fear, doubt or hesitancy. These feelings were generated from familiarity from instances when you set out to make changes, but the changes failed to stick. Resistance is to be expected, you're human after all. The key to lasting change is how you respond to the resistance and the roadblocks — do you give in, give up or feel the discomfort and push through? Imagine a tiny seed planted in the ground. Given water and nutrients, it begins to grow, but first it must break through the resistance of the outer shell, and then the soil, until finally it breaks through the ground and grows tall. Anytime you face change, doubt or uncertainty, remember the seed. Push through the resistance...grow tall and see what's on the other side.

Below is an illustration of all the factors that might be standing in your way of success: fear, doubt, limiting beliefs, excuses and the list goes on. In order to overcome the external pressures, you must create an antidote to keep you moving forward and fend off anything that could cause you to falter. That antidote is a strong internal drive.

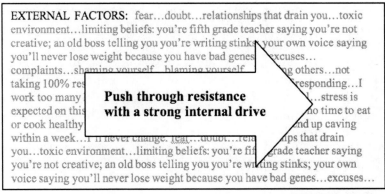

EXTERNAL FACTORS: fear...doubt...relationships that drain you...toxic environment...limiting beliefs: you're fifth grade teacher saying you're not creative; an old boss telling you you're writing stinks; your own voice saying you'll never lose weight because you have bad genes...excuses... complaints...shaming yourself, blaming yourself...blaming others...not taking 100% res... responding...I work too many... stress is expected on this... no time to eat or cook healthy... nd up caving within a week...I'll never change. fear...doubt...rela... ps that drain you...toxic environment...limiting beliefs: you're fif... rade teacher saying you're not creative; an old boss telling you you're writing stinks; your own voice saying you'll never lose weight because you have bad genes...excuses...

Push through resistance with a strong internal drive

© 2011 Thrive 9 to 5®

Generating a strong internal drive demands a close look at the beliefs you keep, the thoughts you think and the outcomes you're currently yielding. It's also about pushing through resistance and boundaries to create a new comfort zone.

We all know that change isn't always easy because our natural tendency is to slip back into our old comfort zone. Success coach and author Robert MacPhee defines the comfort zone as the place "when the results we get are in alignment with our beliefs about who we are."[3] MacPhee concludes that we have two choices when it comes to our comfort zone:

1. Stop taking the actions that are creating the desired result (keep the status quo) or;
2. Change your belief about who you really are (create a new comfort zone).

Choose #1 and you keep your current mindset, stop taking action and slip back into your comfort zone. You also keep the same results. This is what happens when you start a new, healthy routine, but don't believe you're worthy of the results: your new habits fail to stick.

Keep thinking what you're thinking and it will come true. The principles of the law of attraction state that with every thought, you send out an energetic vibration to the universe. Your thoughts determine the outcomes in your life. If you're thinking you can't do something, you are not worthy or you have doubts, you're telling the world you can't do it. And the world will respond exactly as you think: you won't achieve it.

Choose #2 and you create a new mindset and comfort zone with new results. Anticipate and be ready for a little bit of discomfort as you "up level" your life, but good change will come as a product of your strong internal drive. Your beliefs and thoughts drive your actions and determine your results.

All winners want a greater level of success. Read on for how to create a new mindset and comfort zone.

Unleash Your "Inner Advertiser"SM for a Winning Mindset

Imagine an inner dialogue so strong and resilient that you could assimilate external messages and negative self-talk without disrupting your self-esteem or getting thrown off track. Your "Inner Advertiser"SM is the solution — the positive, affirmative voice that aligns with your true desires and will catapult you to greater success, health and happiness. Combat the destructive cacophony with a glorious symphony of inner advertisements that support you — affirming thoughts, supportive beliefs and an "I can do it, anything is possible" attitude.

In this section, you will discover how to unleash your *inner advertiser* and, with it quickly identify negative self-talk and thoughts and either annihilate them or transform them into powerful affirmations for success. You will break the endless loop of negativity by changing your self-talk and your self-image to accelerate desired performance change.

The degree of your negative self-talk does not matter. Whether you were raised in a negative environment where your parents said you would never succeed, or you were praised as a queen your whole life, the inner advertiser strategy will only strengthen your resolve. Most of us have at least one or two damaging voices from our past that still echo in our heads: the third grade teacher saying, "You're not creative," or an old boss telling you, "You can't write." It's time to edit them out of your life's script.

The first step in creating a strong inner dialogue is generating awareness of your current self-talk. With awareness, you can change the filter through which you experience the world and transform your results. Then you will turn those negative statements to positive affirmations.

In order to rewire your brain and reverse the brainwashing of harmful messages, you need to create and repeat your own inner advertising. What are the messages that boost your self-confidence and enthusiasm? What thoughts help remove the charge from external influences and help you respond to situations instead of react? Your truth statements become affirmations for creating the life you want. You can be successful in your career and still take care of yourself; the two are not mutually exclusive. You can find the time, the energy and the focus once you drop your resistance and eliminate the lies you tell yourself. There is always another option and you always have the choice to explore.

Here are a couple of examples to get you warmed up. Once you tune into the voice in your head, you will realize there's a lot more chatter going on up there than you thought!

Your Beliefs and Thoughts About Your Health
You set a goal to lose 10 pounds. You step on the scale after one week and you've gained one pound. How do you react? What do you say to yourself?

_____
_____
_____

You vowed to start eating healthy on Monday and attend an office birthday party on Wednesday. You indulge in a piece of cake. What are you saying to yourself before, during and after the slice?

_____
_____
_____

It's Friday morning, and you hit snooze on your alarm clock for the fifth time this week, instead of getting out of bed to exercise. Describe your self-talk as you hit snooze.

_____

_____

_____

Can you be a healthy, vibrant being even though you gained one pound, had a piece of cake or hit the snooze button? Or are you beating yourself up, frustrated at your inability to achieve results and your immediate willingness to cave into temptations that come your way? What does your reaction tell you about your core belief about who you are? Does that reaction generate energy or rob you of energy? How can you speak your truth with integrity?

Your Thoughts and Beliefs About Your Work

It's been a crazy month and you are exhausted and stressed beyond your limits. Your boss drops another four-hour project on your desk, just as you were getting ready to wrap up for the evening. How do you react?

_____

_____

_____

Can you still be a dedicated, committed employee and state your truth, even if you wind up taking the project anyway? Or do you accept it with a smile, then break into a rage or tears once the boss leaves, and curse underneath your breath working away for the next four hours? What does your reaction tell you about your core belief about who you are? Does that reaction generate or rob you of energy?

Transform Destructive Thoughts

Now, let's identify your own destructive thoughts by taking a hard look at what you are really saying. Then we'll transform them into affirmative statements. Follow these three steps and list your answers on the guide on the following pages:

1. Throughout the day, keep track of the statements and thoughts you keep repeating to yourself that aren't serving you. Write them down.
2. Read each one and ask yourself, "What am I really saying about myself?"
3. Ask yourself, "How is that a lie?" Rewrite the script and rephrase the statement as the truth.

Here are a few examples:

Negative self-talk: I'll never lose weight for the long term. I diet for a while and then gain it all back. It's no use.
What I'm saying: I have no willpower and I'll never succeed. I'm not strong enough and I'm a failure.
The Truth: I am a healthy and vibrant person.

Negative self-talk: I don't have time to exercise.
What I'm saying: My physical health is not important enough to me to find the time. I'm not important. I have no control over my time.
The Truth: I am a healthy and vibrant person and I find time to exercise.

Negative self-talk: I'm completely overwhelmed at the amount of work I have to do and I don't know where to begin.
What I'm saying: I have no control; external factors dictate my workday. I'm in over my head, again.
The Truth: I have the strength and poise to get through this. I know I have options — I can ask for help, delegate, push back or wave the white flag in despair. I will prevail.

Write your statements here:

My Negative Self-Talk:
_____

What I'm Saying:
_____

My Truth:
_____

My Negative Self-Talk:
_____

What I'm Saying:
_____

My Truth:
_____

My Negative Self-Talk:
_____

What I'm Saying:
_____

My Truth:
_____

My Negative Self-Talk:
_____

What I'm Saying:
_____

My Truth:
_____

Change Your Self-Image & Outlook with Affirmations

"Change begins with the belief of who you are." — *Robert MacPhee, President and Founder of Heart Set, Inc. and author of Manifesting for Non-Gurus*

With each lie that you tell yourself, you're also weakening your self-image and the opportunity to achieve the results you desire. Who are you and who do you need to become to achieve your goals? Are your current beliefs and thoughts supporting this image?

Consider the years of pre-conditioning that impact your current mindset. Beliefs that you adopted or assimilated from your culture, society and/or your family may be halting your success. Pinpoint any voices from your past telling you "You can't do that," or "You'll never succeed," "You'll never lose weight," or "You're not creative." Now is the time to rewrite your history on your own terms. Your success depends on it.

Here are some additional truth messages to help you own the experience and empower yourself to achieve greater levels of success in your life. The list includes statements that focus on who you are and what you believe to be true. Read through them and circle the statements that resonate best with you. What are new thoughts you want to think? What are some new beliefs about yourself that you want to adopt? Circle as many as you like.

I am....
- I am healthy and vibrant.
- I am an expert in my field.
- I am a trusted mentor.
- I am innovative and creative.
- I am valued and appreciated wherever I go.
- I effortlessly share my wisdom, insight and expertise with my colleagues and provide incredible value to the organization.
- I am incredibly successful.
- I am totally confident and certain in my career, health and life decisions.
- I am a powerful, resourceful creator attracting all the opportunities I want and need.

- I am honest, honorable and act with integrity.
- I am worthy of the very best in my life and am now willing to allow it.
- I was born with potential.
- I am committed, determined and passionate about what I do.
- I am a very focused and persistent leader.
- I am a smart and savvy business person.
- I am uniquely talented to achieve all of my goals.
- I am prepared for the future.
- I am so grateful for the success I am now achieving.

My work...
- I live each day with passion and purpose.
- I respect my abilities and I consistently fulfill my potential.
- I deserve happiness and prosperity.
- Giving excellent service to my clients/customers brings me great abundance.
- I have great ideas.
- All of my work is of the highest quality.
- People love doing business with me.
- I consistently provide value to my clients and my customers.

Challenges...
- I have faith in myself and the process I am going through.
- Obstacles or any mistakes I make are merely stepping stones on my pathway.
- Life brings me everything I need for my next step.
- I bless the gift of disappointment.
- It is easy for me to embrace change.
- I now release any overload or frustration that I may be feeling.

I have what I need to succeed...
- My life is now filled with prosperity and abundance.
- I allow myself to think big dreams.
- I have tremendous energy and focus for achieving all my goals.

- I now have all the tools and resources to fulfill all of my health and career goals.
- Life brings me everything I need for my next step.
- I express gratitude for everything in my life.
- I prosper wherever I turn.
- I am always in the right place at the right time.
- Today I create a new life, with new principles and standards that totally support me.
- I choose to feel peace in this moment, rather than stress, fear, uncertainty or (fill in the blank).
- I now have complete freedom over my time.
- I pay attention to my needs and how to fulfill them.
- I have my own voice, easily express my thoughts and always trust my intuition.

Start rewiring your mindset now and replace your self-limiting beliefs with these affirmations.

If your first response when reading the statement is to laugh or say "no way," rephrase it to make it work for you, or create your own. The exercise of repeating positive statements will only result in positive feelings if you believe they're true. Ask yourself: "Does this thought make me feel good?" "No." "Well how about this thought?" "Not really." "Here's another." When you hear messages from colleagues, family or friends, ask: "Does this expectation match up with my own?" If not, learn how to identify the "untruths" and replace them with your own beliefs.

Copy your statements on a note card and keep them in your wallet, at your desk or near your nightstand, etc. Make the intention to read your statements and repeat them to yourself regularly.

You can also record them on an audio file and add them to your playlist on your iPod. For a more powerful impact to quickly rewire your mind, supplement your audio track with baroque music. Studies show that classical music activates your alpha brain waves,[4] which means your subconscious mind picks up the statements and adopts them as truth, even if your conscious mind still doubts their truth.

Excuses, Excuses. Raise Your Standards Now!

Excuses are reasons or explanations put forward to defend or justify a fault or offense. When you're on the journey to thrive, excuses become obstacles to success. For every blame, shame or excuse, you take your eye off the ball.

Where are you being distracted or depleted by excuses or justifications? When it comes to making healthy changes to our routine, excuses abound everywhere. Here are some common excuses in the workplace routine:

"I don't have time." If you could improve how you approach your tasks or how you do spend your time, would you find time to get healthy or decrease your stress?

"My job is too important, health isn't a priority right now." Of course your job is important. But working yourself to the point of burnout or illness will have a negative impact on your long-term performance and vitality. World-class athletes embrace rest and recovery after intense periods of training. Being healthy doesn't have to be all or nothing. A tiny break or indulgence in self-care during the work day can get you back on track.

"I have to eat/drink what they serve." We blindly accept the notion that we have to drink alcohol at client/business functions and office happy hours even though we know that one alcoholic beverage can lead to two or three and endless munching on greasy, fried and fattening snacks all night long. We think we have to eat the steak and potatoes dinner at 9 pm three nights a week, and of course, accept the dessert. It's just part of the game. What would happen if you challenged these beliefs and started making healthier choices?

"I deserve a treat." You work hard. Yet ask yourself, how many treats have you had today or this week? Start noticing when the treats and the "I deserve it" excuse become a usual part of your routine.

"I don't need to be concerned about headaches, bellyaches and almost-fainting shakes." These are not normal symptoms you have to or should tolerate. What's the source behind these issues? Find out and quit remedying your ailments with band-aids and pill popping.

"There are too many temptations and I'm weak, so I cave in." Identify the temptations and pitfalls and design strategies to combat them. When

and where are you the weakest? Racing to the vending machine at 3 pm or grabbing the Friday morning donuts? Decide how you can set yourself up for success and create stronger boundaries.

"I never follow through on new, healthy routines." Redefine success. What if success wasn't about the drudgery or misery of following a diet or exercise regime? Redefine success on your own terms. Perhaps it means following through on one healthy habit each day, enjoying one more serving of fruit during the day, 10 minutes on the treadmill or walking the stairs...you decide.

Eliminate Your Excuses

Excuses become obstacles to success. Quit blaming someone else or something else and take back control. You and only you are 100 percent responsible for your life. Live and work to a higher set of standards.

What excuses do you need to get rid of?

_____

_____

_____

Where can you raise your standards?

_____

_____

_____

Where can you set better boundaries — what do you need to stop doing and to whom do you need to say no?

_____

_____

_____

How can you raise your work-life standards? List the actions you want to continue doing, stop doing or start doing. Keep a running list; we'll be exploring more about your habits in Part 3.

Continue or Start Doing   Stop Doing

_____   _____
_____   _____
_____   _____
_____   _____
_____   _____

The Power of Detachment

A lack of willpower is no longer a valid excuse for failure. The good news is that a strong internal drive doesn't run on willpower or muscling your way through. In fact, too much willpower is harmful to progress and can get you stuck. The white-knuckle approach to any task causes pain and discomfort. You expend so much energy, but aren't making any progress. Eventually, over time, you become comfortable with your white knuckles, expending energy and not getting anywhere.

Try this exercise: Make the strongest fist you can muster and hold it for 90 seconds. If you've got nails, you'll feel them cutting into your palm. After a minute, you'll start to feel comfortable. It's not so bad, right? You find comfort in the discomfort.

Getting stuck in the yearning, wanting something so bad, willing so hard for something to happen and trying too hard all create resistance. And what you resist persists. Yearn and the result you get is to keep yearning. Want and you keep wanting. Try harder and you keep trying harder. You feel like a human in the hamster wheel chasing your goals, only to generate feelings of lack and unworthiness. And the results always lie outside of your reach.

Break the cycle of obsessing and create your best reality by not trying so hard. That's right. It's time to release the white-knuckle grip and all of the emotions that accompany it. Swap out obsession for detachment. Know where you want to go, take the action, but drop the drama. Exit the hamster wheel and jump in the inner tube in the river and go with the flow.

Release the tight grip on your thoughts altogether. Easier said then done, I know. Incessant thoughts fill our mind all day long. And we tend to hold on tightly to things we really want and those that we don't want. Use your own releasing technique, or exploring existing methods such as The Sedona Method®, The Work of Byron Katie® or the emotional freedom technique®/EFT[5], to help you ease the tight grip you hold on your thoughts and emotions. Anytime the grip is tight, you create resistance. Again, what you resist, persists. Therefore, you can want a goal so badly that you're actually creating resistance and suffering and limiting yourself from achieving it.

When you are clear about who you are, what you want, take appropriate action and act as if you already achieved it, your inner drive magically steers the raft and you're in a much stronger place to ride the rapids that may take you off course. You're in a much better position to distance yourself from negative thoughts and emotions. Sure you'll still experience them, but they won't stop you in your tracks.

Chapter Summary

✓ Your Thrive 9 to 5® Mindset is your framework for thinking that empowers you to generate a strong internal drive for greater motivation and productivity. The stronger your internal drive, the better you can manage all of the external influences that might be pulling you off track.

✓ Actions produce results, and the more effective your actions, the better the results. But there's another critical link in the equation that is often overlooked in the business world: beliefs and thoughts drive actions.

✓ You have considerable control and choice over what you think and how you act.

✓ False beliefs, negative thoughts and destructive self-talk can act as barriers to success and limit the valuable energy you need to reach potential. Generating a strong internal drive demands a close look at the thoughts you think, the beliefs you keep and the outcomes you're currently yielding. It's also about pushing through resistance and boundaries to create a new comfort zone.

✓ Creating a strong inner dialogue entails rewiring your beliefs and thoughts to reverse harmful messages. Generate awareness for your lies, false beliefs and excuses. Unleash your Inner AdvertiserSM, or series of inner advertisements, to transform negative self-talk and supportive affirmations. What are the messages that boost your self-confidence and resolve? What thoughts help remove the charge from external influences and help you respond to situations instead of react? Your truth statements help you create the life you want.

Take Action Challenge

List your top five affirmations — the truth statements you need to hear to start rewiring your mindset for success.

1._____
2._____
3._____
4._____
5._____

Chapter Conclusion

In the next chapter, you will shift from mindset to habits. Part III provides tips and techniques to improve your energy, adaptability, focus and purpose.

Part III

The Thrive 9 to 5® Workstyle

4

Your Thrive 9 to 5® Workstyle

In the previous section, we discovered the key elements that make up your Thrive 9 to 5® Mindset and specifically the beliefs and thoughts that drive your performance. In this section, we will focus on your workstyle — the habits, behaviors and actions of your daily routine and the standards by which you work.

And similar to the approach in the last section, you will generate awareness for the elements of your workstyle that serve you and eliminate those that do not serve you. The chapters in this section include:

- Chapter 5: Energy
- Chapter 6: Tips to Thrive/Eating for Energy
- Chapter 7: Adaptability
- Chapter 8: Tips to Thrive/Stress-Busting Strategies
- Chapter 9: Focus
- Chapter 10: Purpose

Review your Thrive 9 to 5® Workstyle score in Chapter 2. Are there certain areas you'd like to work on first? Skip ahead to those chapters. And come back to the others, or read through each chapter and carefully to pick up strategies and tools to help you thrive at work.

Once you've identified your new workstyle, you'll move on to Part IV to create a clear roadmap for where you want to go, identify measurable goals to track your progress and create a 90-day action plan to put it to work!

The first stop in your Thrive 9 to 5® Workstyle: assessing your energy levels.

5

Energy

Energy is the secret elixir to your success. It is the magic ingredient that will help you achieve more, be more and do more in your professional and personal life. Energy — and generating more of it — is at the core of our quest for living life to its fullest and feeling better about the journey.

We all want more energy — that positive feeling that ignites passion, excitement and enthusiasm in our lives. More energy in the morning — so you jump out of bed with vigor for life, ready to tackle the day; more energy during the workday—so you greet your colleagues with a smile and apply a "no problem, can do" attitude towards every task that is thrown your way; more energy in the late afternoon — so you can wrap up your workday and head home with a smile on your face, excited to whip up dinner and enjoy the evening with your spouse, children or friends; and more energy on the weekends to tackle mundane errands with joy and experience rest and rejuvenation. We are all looking to tap an energy source that keeps us flying on a natural high, propels us to live life to its fullest and achieve everything we dream. But how often do you experience high-energy days where nothing seems to get you down and you feel great all day long?

How many times in your busy day do you tap sources of energy that don't serve you? The supposed "pick-me-ups" — excessive caffeine, highly-processed foods, refined sugars and nutrient-void snacks — that leave you crashing and burning minutes later. While they taste good going down and feel great at the onset, an hour later you're left depleted and lethargic. Ditto for the non-food triggers: getting wrapped up in office drama, stress-filled reactions and distractions that steer you off course.

Yet how can you expect to perform at optimal levels on a diet of caffeine and stress? When you put junk in your body and put up with drama, you're sabotaging yourself. When you stay up all night and consistently rob yourself of rest, you're really adding more hours to every task in front of you. You're sabotaging your efficiency, your effectiveness and ultimately your productivity. You're also fogging your brain, intuition and creativity. When you operate on a diet of caffeine, sugar and junk food, you're starving your brain and limiting the speed and depth to which you can work. It's as though someone has reined you in with a harness, tied your hands behind your back and you downshifted your brain to a slower gear.

Often we've been in this cycle for so long that we don't know the difference. We don't even know what it's like to operate at an optimal level.

The quality of the energy you put towards your work is more important than the number of hours you are logging. Yet how many of us spin our wheels in a whirlwind of "busy-ness" and end the day in despair because we didn't accomplish much?

Most of us move fast through life and the work day, multi-tasking, checking off to-dos. We operate at full throttle, full time, often at the risk of our own health. We are demanding of our bodies and minds, yet feed ourselves garbage and treat ourselves with little care. We skim off the top because we don't have the energy to go deeper, pay more attention or give more focus. We start to feel sluggish and nearly doze off at our desks. We're not engaged and are easily distracted. We're impatient and bear an increasingly negative attitude. We lack connectivity to ourselves, our colleagues and our mission. We lack passion. The cost of mindless working is tragic: We lose our edge and creativity while complacently stoking the fires of mediocrity.

When you feel better and have more energy — enough to walk around all day grinning from ear to ear (or at least smiling inside) and giving 100 percent effort towards everything on your plate during and outside of work — you are more productive, have a greater ability to focus, are a more pleasant person and ultimately feel good about yourself while improving the bottom line.

Generating more energy during your day can help you improve your:
- *Motivation and drive to get the job done and provide the enthusiasm and vigor to keep you immersed in your work.* You feel inspired and empowered to take initiative and go beyond what's expected.

- *Physical strength and stamina, staying power (tenacity to see things through) and physical health.* You feel great and experience fewer headaches, backaches, sinus infections, cloudy head, allergies, stomachaches, heartburn, etc.
- *Mental acuity, creativity, innovation and decision-making.* You experience greater mental clarity and the ability to generate ideas and problem solve.
- *Focus and efficiency, as well as ability to be succinct and concise.* You know what you're doing and why you're doing it instead of meandering or wasting time.
- *Self-confidence and esteem.* You believe in yourself and limit hesitancy and ambivalence.
- *Engagement and involvement.* You feel connected to tasks, goals and teammates.
- *Equanimity, balance and consistency.* You respond with a level head, operating from a place of measured response instead of knee-jerk reaction or out of control drama.

So, Where Do I Find This Magical Energy?

Unfortunately, there is no one-size-fits-all silver bullet that will work for everybody. We each have a unique biochemistry: body shape, size, age, blood type, genetics, ancestry, metabolism, etc. Therefore, what works for your colleague may not work for you.

But rest assured, a silver bullet does exist and it's yours and yours alone. With a little excavation, you can define it for yourself. In this chapter, you tune into your body and mind and become acutely aware of your energizers and energy drains to discover your silver bullet to increased vitality. Learn to identify which habits and behaviors to eliminate and which to keep.

Energy Defined

The definition of energy is "the capacity for vigorous activity; available power and the exertion of such power." However, we each have our own interpretation of what that means in our daily lives.

It's important to get clear about your personal definition. The clearer you are about what you want, the more likely you are to create it and make it your reality. Take a few moments to answer these questions:

1. What does having more energy mean to you?

   _____
   _____
   _____

2. What type of energy do you want?

   _____
   _____
   _____

3. Why do you want it?

   _____
   _____
   _____

4. What would you do with more energy that you're not currently doing?

   _____
   _____
   _____

5. How will your work, life and relationships improve?

   _____
   _____
   _____

Take the Five-Day Energy Challenge

The next step is to uncover your unconscious habits and tune into what energizes you, what drains you during your day and where you can find more energy. By generating awareness, you can then identify what needs to change, where you can add more energizers and where you need to plug the holes that drain your precious energy. Making the critical link between your habits and their impact on your performance can be an eye opener.

For the next five work days, keep track of your energy levels throughout the day and evening. Notice when you feel like you're on fire — full of energy and ready to tackle the world — and when you feel like you could crawl under the desk and take a nap. At the end of each day, write down what fueled you and what drained you.

Your fuel could be from food and drink, positive interactions with others, actions and successes or positive thoughts and beliefs.

Your drains could be from the quick fixes, such as sugar and junk food rushes that give you an immediate boost but leave you lethargic within an hour. You also may be losing energy from the people, actions and things that you are tolerating.

Below are templates to help you track your energy levels. They include a daily grid to track your energy during the day and charts to use at the end of the week, summarizing your energy drains and energizers. Free copies of the templates are available for you to download at http://www.thrive9to5.com/journal.php.

Your Daily Energy Flow

On a scale of 0 – 10 (0 = pure exhaustion and eyelids closing; 10 = bouncing off the wall), rank your energy levels periodically throughout the day. Start by marking dots at the appropriate levels. At the end of the day, connect the dots. Use Chart 5-1 as a template.

Daily Energy Levels						
High 10						
9						
8						
7						
6						
5						
4						
3						
2						
1						
Low 0						
	6:00 AM	9:00 AM	12:00 PM	3:00 PM	6:00 PM	9:00 PM
	Time of Day					
Notes						

Energy Level (vertical axis label)

Chart 5-1

What did you eat or drink during the day that fueled you? Drained you?

_____

_____

_____

What actions or interactions with others fueled you? Drained you? What do you need to ask for? Where do you need to say no?

_____

_____

_____

Chapter 5: Energy

What incomplete actions or messes need to be addressed? For example, are there tasks you just couldn't get to or actions that have been on your to-do list for three months? *(Most likely, these items are draining you.)*

_____
_____
_____

What thoughts and beliefs do you need to change? Do you spend part of your day complaining, blaming, whining, shaming or guilting yourself? *(These actions all erode your precious energy.)*

_____
_____
_____

What habits do you need to "up level" (nutrition, exercise, stress management)?

_____
_____
_____

How can you choose to respond instead of knee-jerk reacting?

_____
_____
_____

Where can you clean up your environment (physical space)?

_____
_____
_____

What do you need to ask for to help boost your energy or be more productive?

_____
_____
_____

Where do you need to start saying no and draw stronger boundaries?

_____

_____

_____

Weekly Summary

At the end of the week, compare your findings from the five days. Jot down your notes in the Weekly Summary (See Chart 5-2) and identify what drained you, what fueled you and new habits you want to adopt.

Weekly Summary

	What drained me?	What fueled me?	What needs to change or continue?
Physical: food, drink, sleep, exercise			
Emotional: reactions to people, situations; my thoughts or beliefs			
Successful actions; inactions or incomplete actions			
My environment			

Chart 5-2

Are there any surprises?

_____

_____

_____

Are your energy levels consistent from day to day?

_____
_____
_____

What time of the day do you experience peak energy? Does that correlate to your current work routine and schedule?

_____
_____
_____

What similarities do you see in your fuelers and drainers?

_____
_____
_____

Chapter Summary

- ✓ Generating more energy during your day can help you improve your motivation, enthusiasm, stamina, mental acuity, focus, self-esteem and consistency. What does having more energy mean to you?

- ✓ The key to finding more energy in your day is to pinpoint what fuels you and what drains you in your current routine. Your fuel could be from food and drink, positive interactions with others, actions and successes or positive thoughts and beliefs. Your drains could be from the quick fixes, such as sugar and junk food rushes that give you an immediate boost, but leave you lethargic within an hour. You also may be losing energy from the people, actions and things that you are tolerating.

- ✓ What in your daily routine do you want to keep doing, stop doing or start doing?

Take Action Challenge

List your 10 priority energizers and drainers and keep them visible as daily reminders to help identify what to include and what to avoid.

Top Fuelers

1._____
2. _____
3. _____
4. _____
5. _____

Top Drainers

6. _____
7. _____
8. _____
9. _____
10. _____

Repeat the exercises in this chapter any time you feel yourself slipping back into an unconscious routine or when you find yourself completely exhausted. Let your awareness become the catalyst for changing your behavior.

Chapter Conclusion

Now that you've generated awareness for your energizers and drainers, put them to work for you. Keep this awareness to fine tune your actions. The next chapter provides more tips and strategies focused on eating for energy.

6

Tips to Thrive/Eating for Energy

The clock strikes 3 pm and — as if on cue — your energy evaporates with your next exhale. Perhaps you experience a tiny grumble emerging from deep inside your core. But if you indulged in a carb-feeding frenzy at noon, that grumble erupts into a roar and you find yourself face-to-face with a full-fledged sugar crash. You are at the bottom of a deep, dark pit helplessly gazing up, and that empty cavern you call a stomach needs food, fast.

Add to the mix a deadline due by 5 pm, and no doubt you are going to grab whatever food item is in sight in order to claw your way back to satiety...a candy bar...a soda...or you might even take a 10-minute trot around the block for a sugar-laden treat. At this point in your afternoon, bad snack options begin to look really good. At any other time, you know that junk food spells danger and you turn your nose up and walk away. But those are the times when you have plenty of energy. When you are desperate for a lift and under stress, you start making excuses, "Oh, it's just a little treat." "I don't have time for anything else." You don't even realize that your brain is a bit cloudy, and your ravenous instincts are trying to talk you straight up and down another sugar spike. Now is a great time for a little food psychology.

Brian Wansink, Director of the Cornell Food and Brand Lab and author of *Mindless Eating*, concludes that people eat whatever is in sight, and the closer the food item, the more likely they will indulge. In his research, Wansink monitored the snacking habits of office workers — some had candy bowls on their desks, others on credenzas a few steps away. Those who had the candy within arm's length snacked more. Why? It was pure convenience. He also compared how many hands reached into a clear candy dish vs. a solid colored dish. The results? Hands are more apt to dig in when the eyes can see what they are grabbing. So fill those clear bowls with fruits and good snacks!

This chapter includes tips and techniques to set yourself up for success so you are eating for long-lasting energy throughout the day.

Healthy Eating Strategies of Highly Successful People

Defend yourself against the diet destroyers in the office and arm yourself for success. Preparation is a critical element for the battle. Remember, your primal instincts won't help you climb out of the bottomless hunger pit. Make it easy on yourself and keep healthy options convenient. Here are 10 strategies to jump start your energy during the day.

Strategy #1: Grab-and-Go Breakfasts
Here are 10 grab-and-go breakfast options that are quick and painless:
1. Instant plain oatmeal topped with fresh apple slices and cinnamon.
2. Plain Greek yogurt and a couple of slivered almonds. (Check your yogurt labels for sugar content; plain yogurt brands tend to have less sugar).
3. Egg whites to go. Crack 2 egg whites in pan; cook for 5-7 minutes; season with salt and pepper.
4. Protein shake. Shake or blend two scoops of your favorite protein mix with water, nonfat milk or dairy alternatives and ice.
5. A tablespoon of peanut butter on a whole-wheat toast with sliced banana.
6. A snack bag filled with walnuts, almonds, raisins or other dried fruit.
7. Hummus on ½ pumpernickel bagel.
8. Smoked salmon, slice of tomato, capers, smeared lightly with cream cheese on pumpernickel bread.
9. Soft goat cheese on a whole-wheat pita.
10. Grab-and-go breakfast bar. Look for bars with at least 4 grams of fiber, 5 grams of protein and no more than 8 grams of sugar per serving.

Strategy #2: Power Up on Protein

Eating more protein will boost your alertness and energy. Judith Wurtman, a professor at the Massachusetts Institute of Technology (MIT), researched how certain foods alter one's mood by influencing the level of certain brain chemicals. Wurtman reported that people are more alert when their brains are producing the neurotransmitters dopamine and norepinephrine.[6] These two important brain chemicals that appear to be influenced by foods, produce an increased ability to concentrate, and faster reaction times. Both dopamine and norepinephrine are synthesized from the amino acid tyrosine, which can be found in almonds, avocados, beans, pumpkin and mustard seeds. Other foods high in protein include:

Food	Serving	Protein Grams[7]
Cottage cheese, (lowfat, 1% milkfat)	1 cup	28
Endamame	1 cup	22
Shaklee's Cinch® meal-in-a bar	1 bar	20
Skim milk	1 cup	8
Cheddar cheese	1 ounce	7
Stonyfield Farm Organic Yogurt (plain)	6 ounce container	7
Almonds, dry roasted	1 ounce	6
Hummus	1/3 cup	6
Walnuts (raw)	1 ounce	4
Quaker Instant Oatmeal	1 packet (prepared with water)	3

Strategy #3: Fuel Up on Fiber

Fiber is a miracle nutrient that increases satiety (the feeling of fullness), dampens hunger and reduces caloric intake. According to the Institute of Medicine's Food and Nutrition Board, which establishes principles and guidelines for adequate nutrition, women should consume 21 grams of fiber a day and men, 30 grams. Make sure you are getting a good dose of fiber during your afternoon snack time. Here are a few tips to add more fiber to your diet:

- Scan for bran — look for labels that contain bran and whole-wheat as the first ingredients.
- Grab the whole food — one medium orange contains three grams of fiber. One 8-ounce cup of orange juice with pulp contains 0 percent.[8]
- Savor the skins — apple, pear and plum skins contain fiber and other nutrients. Just be sure to buy organic to enjoy pesticide-free skins.
- Opt for bean spreads — think hummus.
- Bite a berry or two — choose raspberries, blackberries or dates for an afternoon snack. They have twice the fiber of many other fruit selections. Fiber ratings for fruit options include:

Food	Serving	Grams of Fiber[9]
Figs (dried)	1 cup	15
Dates	1 cup	12
Blackberries	1 cup	8
Raspberries	1 cup	8
Dried cranberries	1 cup	6
Kiwi	1 cup	5
Apple (with skin)	1 medium	4
Blueberries	1 cup	4
Pear (with skin)	1 medium	4
Orange	1 medium	3
Grapefruit (pink, white or red)	1 cup (with juice)	3
Banana	1 medium	3
Cherries (sweet)	1 cup	3
Strawberries	1 cup	3
Cantaloupe	1 cup (balls)	2
Peach	1 medium	2
Nectarine	1 small	2
Mango	1 cup (sliced)	2
Pineapple	1 cup (chunks)	2
Raisins	Small box	2
Grapes (seedless)	1 cup	1
Watermelon	1 cup	1

Strategy #4: Rethink Your Drink

Packing on the pounds or running on fumes at work? The culprit could be in your cup. Do you mindlessly drink soda, sweetened tea, vitamin water or other sugary drinks throughout the day? Or hit the coffee shop for a frothy, whip-creamed-topped beverage? Drinkers beware. Know the calorie, caffeine and sugar content of your drinks.

The caffeine content in an 8-ounce cup of regular coffee from 100-200 milligrams; 16-ounce cup (usually medium size), 266 milligrams; and one ounce of espresso, 75 milligrams. According to the staff at the MayoClinic, "moderate caffeine intake isn't likely to cause harm but too much can noticeably affect your health. Heavy daily caffeine use — more than 500 to 600 mg a day, or about four to seven cups of coffee — can cause insomnia, nervousness, restlessness, irritability, headaches and anxiety."[10] Pay attention to your caffeine intake and know how much you can safely consume daily without experiencing these side effects. Also, if you enjoy a late afternoon or evening caffeinated beverage, make sure it's not robbing you of precious sleep.

Keep your eye on the sugar content and remember, one gram of sugar equals 4 teaspoons. So if you have a daily habit of drinking one 8-ounce cola a day that means almost 10 teaspoons of sugar! Here are some suggestions to help you rethink your drink for more long-lasting energy:

Bag the bean after lunch. Substitute your afternoon cup of coffee for green or black tea to help you remain calm during a hectic day. A study from the University College of London shows that antioxidants in black tea, called catechins, lower levels of the stress hormone cortisol by as much as 20 percent. The National Institutes of Health state that cortisol raises blood pressure and can weaken the immune system. Keep a few tea bags handy to stop you from grabbing that afternoon cup of coffee. If you must add sugar, try honey or agave nectar, natural sweeteners that are low on the glycemic index, and keep blood sugar levels on an even keel.

> **The Glycemic Index (GI)** is a numerical index that ranks carbohydrate-rich foods according to their effect on blood sugar. The higher the number, the greater the crash. So go low.
> The index is a great tool to use to narrow down long-lasting energizing snacks.

Wise up with water. Water is crucial to your health, so drink plenty of it. A glass of H_2O helps absorb the nutrients you consume — including fiber and protein. Water keeps you from dehydrating, which can sap your energy and cause headaches, brain fatigue and muscle weakness. Keep a pitcher of water and a glass nearby and refill often. Natural tea mixes come in handy and have a low calorie count, low sugar and minimal caffeine.

Can the soda for lemon-lime H_2O. High sugar drinks give you a spike, but in the long run may make you sleepier, according to research published in *Human Psychopharmacology: Clinical and Experimental*.[11] Researchers tested volunteers after they consumed either a caffeine- and sugar-free beverage or one with 42 grams of sugar and 30 milligrams of caffeine. Although the sugar and caffeine drinkers experienced improved reaction times and concentration during the first 10 minutes, by the one-hour mark they had slower reaction times and more lapses in concentration than the non-caffeine and non-sugar drinkers. Drop lemon and lime slices in your water pitcher and keep the glass nearby. Sliced cucumber also provides a refreshing twist.

Dilute your fruit juices. If you need a sugar pick-me-up, dilute a glass of all-natural fruit juice. Score a bonus with a glass of grape or cranberry juice. According to a study published in *The American Journal of Clinical Nutrition*, Concord grape juice may lower nocturnal blood pressure and also had a beneficial impact on blood sugar levels compared to flavored drinks.[12] Dilute fruit juices to cut back on the sugar.

Blender buzz. Keep a blender handy and combine your favorite fruits with yogurt, skim milk or ice cubes. Try other dairy alternatives including almond milk, rice milk or coconut water. Add your favorite protein mix for an extra energy punch. Here are a couple tasty combinations that are high in fiber and protein and are great for breakfast, lunch or an afternoon pick-me-up:

> *Berry Bliss:* ½ cup frozen blueberries, 1 cup nonfat plain yogurt, ½ tablespoon of honey and ½ tablespoon of flax seed

> *Banana Blend*: 1 banana, 1 cup nonfat vanilla yogurt, 1/3 cup of 2% milk, 2 cups of ice, pinch of nutmeg and pinch of cinnamon

> *Citrus Blend*: ½ cup peeled, pitted and sliced mango, ½ cup of orange juice; honey to taste and ½ cup of ice

> *Creamsicle Smoothie*: 1 navel orange (peeled), ¼ cup fat-free half-and-half or non-fat yogurt, 2 tablespoons frozen orange juice concentrate, 1/4 teaspoon vanilla extract, ice cubes

> *Pineapple Passion*: 1 cup low-fat or light vanilla yogurt, ice cubes, 1 cup pineapple chunks

> *For more tasty fruit smoothie recipes, visit Prevention Magazine's web site: http://www.prevention.com/smoothies*

Strategy #5: The Desk Drawer Stash

Keep good snack options in your line of sight — on your desk, the bookshelves or even on the window sill. These snacks require no prep time, just remember to pick them up during your next grocery store run. And if you are often on the road, keep a stash in your handbag or your car's glove compartment.

Go nuts. The protein in nuts keeps you satiated. Take a handful, not a bowlful, as nuts are high in calories (from healthy fats).

Walnuts provide heart-healthy omega-3 fatty acids to keep brain cells healthy. A ¼ cup of walnuts or cashews provides 5 grams of protein; the same serving of soy nuts, 11 grams. Combine with raisins or other dried fruit for quick homemade trail mix.

Pack a protein punch. Keep your office drawer stocked with high-protein snack bars, such as Shaklee's Cinch® Meal-In-A-Bar. One meal replacement bar packs 20 grams of protein and stops the light-headedness within seconds. Half a peanut butter sandwich on whole-wheat bread, a banana and a ½ cup of soymilk provides 17 grams of protein.

Sugar, sugar (the natural way). If you need a sugar pick-me-up, opt for fruit. Fresh fruits are naturally rich in fiber, potassium, folate and vitamins C and A. Dried fruit contains fiber and concentrated nutrients, and ½ cup of dried fruit counts as 1 cup of fresh.

Strategy #6: Snag a Corner in the Office Fridge
Stake your own spot in the office refrigerator and keep these healthy staples handy.

Lift the lid and dig in. Keep a week's supply of yogurt for a quick snack. Again, watch the sugar content. Plain and vanilla flavors tend to have much less added sugar. Add fresh fruit, blueberries, strawberries or other seasonal berries that offer non-refined sugars and vitamin C.

Lift the lid and spread. Think hummus on a whole-wheat pita. Garbanzo beans (the main ingredient for hummus) are high in fiber, protein, iron and vitamin C. Two tablespoons of hummus provide 3 grams of protein and 3 grams of fiber, while whole-wheat pitas offer 6 grams of protein and 5 grams of dietary fiber.

More berry bliss. Keep seasonal berries on hand: strawberries, raspberries, blackberries or blueberries. Off season? Try snacking on frozen berries. A good source of vitamin C, berries can help fight a jump in cortisol.

Brown bag it. A stick of string cheese, a slice of whole-wheat bread and a cup of seedless red grapes provide 10 grams of protein and 3 grams of fiber.

Strategy #7: Invest Time on Sunday Evening

Don't have the time to pack your daily snacks at home because your weeknights are jam-packed and the morning minutes escape you as you dash out the door? Then start with baby steps. Take the time on Sunday evening to plan, prepare and pack your meals and snacks for the week…or at least for Monday.

Here are some healthy options that will provide savory flavors and nutrients to satisfy the mid-afternoon hunger pangs.

Energizing Recipes for Your Work Day

Salad with Ginger Carrot Dressing[13]
Prep Time: 5 minutes
For dressing:
1 large carrot, peeled and roughly chopped
1 large shallot, peeled and roughly chopped
2 tablespoons roughly chopped fresh ginger
1 tablespoon sweet white miso
2 tablespoons rice wine vinegar
1 tablespoon roasted sesame seed oil
¼ cup grapeseed oil
2 tablespoons water

For salad:
1 head of baby gem lettuce (or any greens), roughly cut
¼ red onion, thinly sliced
¼ avocado, diced

Pulse the carrot, shallot and ginger in a blender until finely chopped. Scrape down the sides, add the miso, vinegar and sesame seed oil and whiz together. While the blender is going, slowly drizzle in the grapeseed oil and the water. Combine the lettuce, onion and avocado in a salad bowl, drizzle with plenty of dressing and serve.

Guacamole
Time: 10 minutes
2 avocados
Juice of two limes
1 cucumber, peeled, seeded and diced
½ cup chopped cilantro
½ cup cherry tomatoes, halved
Salt and pepper

Mash two avocados in small bowl with the back of a fork. Add lime juice, cucumber, cilantro and tomatoes and mix. Add salt and pepper to taste. Avocados are loaded with B vitamins, which stress quickly depletes and which your body needs to maintain nerves and brain cells. Plus, their creaminess comes from healthy fats. Spread on the goodness!

Broccoli and Arugula Soup[14]
Time: 15 minutes
1 tablespoon olive oil
1 clove garlic, thinly sliced
½ yellow onion, roughly diced
1 head broccoli, cut into small florets (about 2/3 pound)
2½ cups water
¼ teaspoon each coarse salt and freshly ground black pepper
¾ cup arugula (watercress would be good, too)
½ lemon

Heat the olive oil in a medium nonstick saucepan over medium heat. Add the garlic and onion and sauté for just a minute or until fragrant. Add the broccoli and cook for four minutes or until bright green. Add the water, salt and pepper, bring to a boil, lower the heat and cover. Cook for eight minutes or until the broccoli is just tender, add arugula and serve. You can also puree the soup; pour into a blender and puree until quite. Be careful when blending hot liquids; start slowly and work in batches if necessary (you don't want the steam to blow the lid off). Serve the soup with a bit of fresh lemon.

Hummus
Time: 15 minutes
¼ cup plus 1 tablespoon of tahini (ground sesame seeds)
1 19-ounce can of chick peas (garbanzo beans)
Juice of one lemon
2½ tablespoons of olive oil
2½ tablespoons of warm water
3 cloves of garlic
½ teaspoon of salt

Pour everything into a food processor, blend thoroughly. Add more olive oil or water to adjust texture. Serve with carrot sticks, pita bread or your favorite crackers.

Spiced Mixed Nuts
Recipe from Ellie Kreiger's *The Food You Crave*[15]
Time: 20 minutes
½ cup raw pecans
½ cup raw almonds
1/3 cup of shelled raw pistachios
1/3 cup raw cashews
1/3 cup shelled raw pumpkin seeds
1 tablespoon pure maple syrup
1 tablespoon curry powder
Dash of cayenne pepper
½ teaspoon dried rosemary
¼ teaspoon salt
Cooking spray

Preheat oven to 325° F. Combine the nuts and seeds in a medium bowl. Add the maple syrup, spices, rosemary and salt; toss to combine. Coat a baking sheet with cooking spray, then transfer the coated nuts to the sheet and spread evenly in a single layer. Bake, stirring once, until the nuts are fragrant and lightly toasted, 15-20 minutes. Remove from oven and cool. The nuts will keep in an airtight container in the refrigerator for up to two weeks.

Cucumber Couscous

Time: 20 minutes

1 cup whole-wheat couscous

1 tablespoon olive oil

1 cup water

1 cucumber, diced

1 cup cherry tomatoes, quartered

1 lemon (zest and juice)

½ cup of pine nuts

Pour water and olive oil in saucepan, bring to a boil. Remove from heat, add couscous. Cover and let sit for 5 minutes. Place pine nuts on baking sheet and roast in oven; 350° for about 7-10 minutes until lightly browned. After couscous is set, lightly fluff with a fork. Add cucumbers, tomatoes, lemon zest, lemon juice and pine nuts. One cup of whole-wheat couscous provides 8 grams of protein and 7 grams of fiber. Swap couscous with quinoa and you have 5 grams of protein and 3 grams of fiber.

Strategy #8: Experiment With Energizing Grains

Whole grains have been a staple in the human diet since early civilization and are an excellent source of nutrition, as they contain essential enzymes, iron, dietary fiber, vitamin E and B-complex vitamins. Because the body absorbs grains slowly, they provide sustained and high-quality energy. On the down side, they do take time to cook. Therefore, if you have time over the weekend to cook a cup or two of grains, they'll last you the whole week. They're great solo as an energizing breakfast. Add them to vegetables, salads and soups or sprinkle with olive oil for a quick snack. Experiment with these grains and find what provides the best energy for you. Here are basic directions.

1. Measure the grain, rinse in cold water, using a fine mesh strainer. You can soak grains for one hour to soften, increasing digestibility. Drain grains and discard the soaking water.
2. Add grains to recommended amount of water and bring to a boil.
3. Reduce heat, cover and simmer for the time suggested.

1 Cup of Grain	Water	Cooking Time
Amaranth	3 cups	30 minutes
Barley (pearled)	2-3 cups	60 minutes
Brown rice	2 cups	45-60 minutes
Buckwheat (kasha)*	2 cups	20-30 minutes
Bulgur (cracked wheat)	2 cups	20 minutes
Cornmeal (polenta)	3 cups	20 minutes
Couscous (pasta)	1 cup	5 minutes
Millet	2 cups	30 minutes
Quinoa	2 cups	15-20 minutes

Strategy #9: Rate Your Workplace Health

Once you generate awareness about your personal actions and habits, you can then begin to examine your surrounding environments. In the typical work environment, we shrug our shoulders in despair and continue on with daily routines consisting of:

- High-carb lunches and office menus where sugar and carbs are king. Sandwiches, soda, chips and brownies are staples for client meetings, and pizza is required at internal staff meetings or desk-side meals.
- Celebratory treats. Many offices celebrate any success...*every* single milestone...birthdays, engagements, births and company anniversaries. If you work in a large office, that can equate to weekly celebrations with cookies, cakes, brownies, alcohol and other treats.
- Friday morning donuts. Without fail, one of my teammates would bring in the inevitable box of donuts every Friday morning. We worked so hard and so well together, didn't we deserve this sure-fire sugar rush every week?
- Coffee...and not just boring cups of brown liquid. Frothy drinks doused with sugary syrups and topped with mounds of whip cream oozing out of the lid. Anytime you need a jolt, a break or want to procrastinate, coffee is an easy excuse. While city life has its perks, with an average of three coffee stops on each block, there are plenty of them to be found near every suburban office park.

We wonder why our adrenal systems are shot and why day after day our colleagues drop like flies to the flu or even more extreme, to burnout. Living with daily stress on a nutrient-deficient diet wreaks havoc on the body and the brain. Our bodies aren't built to prolong a stressful workstyle over time. At some point, depending on the level of health you are starting with, you will come crashing down.

What are you accepting as status quo that isn't working for you?

Strategy #10: Clean Up Your Workplace and Eliminate Temptations

Take a look around your office and start to pinpoint trouble areas that you can avoid or change. Assess your home environment, too. What changes can you make or who can you ask for help to boost your energy, focus and feeling of calm? Some common areas to look to eliminate office temptations include:

- Desk drawer stashes. What types of snacks do you keep in your desk? Are they healthy (granola bars, nuts, seeds) or are they high-sugar, nutrient-void disasters (chips, cookies, candy)?

- Break rooms. Identify any diet destroyers in your break room. Do you take advantage of the bottled water supply? Refrigerator and microwave for your lunches? How about a blender for healthy shakes and smoothies?

- Vending machines. Do you often raid the vending machines? Are there any nourishing selections (trail mix, nuts, granola bars)?

- Candy bowls. Do you unconsciously raid a colleague's goody bowl when times are tough? What treats are readily accessible to you? How can you limit the temptations for the goodies you crave?

- Meetings. What types of food, snacks and beverages do you choose during office meetings? Are fruits, vegetables and water offered? Are there any healthy alternatives?

- Office parties. What types of food, snacks and beverages do you choose at office parties? Can you make healthier suggestions to your office manager?

- Around the block. Where do you run for lunch or mid-afternoon snack? Do they offer healthy alternatives?

- Food-bearing colleagues Do you have colleagues who continually bring food to the office? Do you easily cave in to the Friday morning donut frenzy? How can you limit the temptation?

- Leftover delights. How often do you receive e-mail alerts from colleagues announcing leftover food in the kitchen? Do you ignore them, or are you first in line to graze the plates?

- Office water cooler. Do your colleagues gather around the water cooler and indulge in gossip? Raise your standards and vow not to partake in conversations that drain your energy and compromise your integrity.

Chapter Summary

✓ Defend yourself against the diet destroyers in the office and arm yourself for success. Preparation is a critical element for the battle. Remember, your primal instincts won't help you climb out of the bottomless hunger pit. Make it easy on yourself and keep healthy options convenient.

- Prepare yourself with grab-and-go breakfasts
- Power up on protein
- Fuel up on fiber
- Rethink your drink
- Arm yourself with a desk drawer and office fridge stash
- Invest time for healthy cooking

✓ Generate awareness about your personal actions and habits and examine your surrounding environments. What are you accepting as status quo that isn't working for you? Clean up your environments and temptations.

Here are four more bonus tips.

✓ **Keep healthy snacks visible:** As Dr. Brian Wansink[16]'s food research concludes, we all tend to succumb to the "see food diet," where we are more likely to eat what we can see. So keep protein, fiber and water in your line of sight.

✓ **Make it convenient:** Put up barriers between you and the vending machine. But light the path between you and the good snacks. And keep your tools handy: an orange peeler, an apple corer and a paring knife will ease the afternoon fruit slicing. Keep the napkins nearby.

✓ **Mother nature tastes best**: Imagine fighting off the temptation of a candy bar and grabbing an orange from the fruit bowl. Your taste buds are on alert and you begin to salivate as you meticulously peel the rind back, only to be sadly disappointed as you bite into the dry, fibrous pith sans flavor or juice. What a waste of time! Make sure you know the seasons for your favorite fruits and veggies, and make sure to buy them when they are ripe and flavorful. Even though our grocery stores sell produce from across the globe year-round, nothing tastes better than a local harvest treat, in season. Crop seasons vary by state, so check your local farmer's market for their harvest schedule. The Fruit Guys (www.fruitguys.com) is an excellent resource for fresh fruit delivered to your office.

✓ **Portion size does matter.** A little protein and fiber go a long way. Snacks such as nuts and granola provide a healthy boost, but too much can lead to trouble with calories and fat content. Keep sushi plates and miniature bowls in your office, so you can hold a handful of nuts or trail mix.

Take Action Challenge

List your top five energizing tips from this chapter and where you know you can raise your standards or improve your environment to support your new energizing routine.

1._____
2._____
3._____
4._____
5._____

Chapter Conclusion

Now that you've tackled the first workstyle element, energy, it's time to move on to the second, adaptability. In the next chapter, you'll discover how improving your flexibility can boost your success and ease your stress.

7

Adaptability

Adaptability is measured by how well you can adjust readily to changing conditions and environments. Your ability to embrace change, bend and bounce back while remaining focused on organizational goals are prized traits in the workplace. Adaptability means you do what it takes to generate the best results. You are able to wear many hats: problem solver, innovator, executer/doer, creator, team member, manager and leader. You can easily toggle among your skillset during the daily flow of operations with ease. You adjust to what's thrown at you and you are proactive, anticipating and trouble-shooting problems. You're coach-able, accepting and incorporating feedback. Your ability to hold the space for greater possibilities and apply a high level of discernment makes you a valuable team member and, ultimately, generates better results for you and your organization.

The most important factor in measuring your adaptability is examining how you respond to situations generated by an unpredictable workflow. If you don't effectively navigate the rocky seas of uncertainty with a cool head and exude grace under pressure, your results are minimized and so is your value. Add to that another byproduct of your inability to be adaptable, flexible and resilient on the job: STRESS!

Losing Your Composure Increases Your Stress Levels

Perhaps you've been pegged as the office drama king or queen. Or you find yourself on one too many occasions losing control or feeling overwhelmed with your workload. No matter the cause, your level of stress and more importantly how you perceive and cope with stress are critical factors determining your state of energy. When you're frazzled, you do not produce your best work.

Yet high risks yield high rewards, so you must be able to handle pressure.

The solution lies in your ability to complement the hard-driving, results-driven demands of the workplace with a composed mindset. Easing stress is determined by:

- How well you recalibrate at the onset of feelings of overwhelm
- How well you greet adversity with persistence and equanimity
- The level of composure to accompany your drive and ambition
- Your ability to be resilient without actively demonstrating the "pain" from the setback

Managing stressful situations begins by changing the way you respond to the situation. Stress is generated from fear: fear of the unknown, fear of not meeting a deadline, fear of not keeping a commitment, fear of _____ (you can fill in the blank). Transform your energy by transforming your thoughts and emotions away from fear and anxiety to tranquility and calm.

Remember, the feelings you experience do not define you. They are just feelings. You can let these feelings go just as easily as you can drop a pen out of your writing hand. Holding on to feelings of stress, lack, doubt or shame only prevent you from having exactly what you want. Whether you choose to hold them for a long time — or whether you choose to release them now is up to you. The choice is yours.

ARR!

That's what I say to stress. I'm not talking about pirates, either. I'm talking about the undeniable fact that your response to any situation dictates your outcome. The formula[17] below explains how.

A — An **action** occurs initiated by you or someone else.

R — You **react.**

R — And you're left with a **result** that you don't like (stress, anxiety, doubt, fear, etc.)

A + R = R!

Think of a recent situation at work where you were less than satisfied, even downright angry or upset with the result. Now, configure this situation as an equation: an action occurred and you reacted to it, delivering the outcome/current situation. As with any equation, if you want a different answer, you need to change one of the factors. And since you have no control over the original action, the only thing left to change is your response to it.

It's critical to note the nuance between reacting vs. responding. Mindless, knee-jerk reactions originate from a place of fear, lack and uncertainty. Responses come from a centered, well-intentioned place of integrity and self-confidence. The good news is that you can choose to respond instead of react to any situation. And you can choose how you respond.

This powerful formula helps you reframe how you look at any aggravating situation in order to immediately relieve the charge, even just a bit. And it focuses on one premise: you don't have control over other people, but you do have control over your own actions and responses. And that is a powerful concept! So for all the drama kings and queens and stressed out, frazzled and doubtful souls, remember: you create your own misery. You also have the power to generate peace and happiness at anytime you wish.

What outcomes are you accepting at work that are less than desirable?

Use this chart to delve deeper and explore your response to each event. Decide how you can change your response to create a more favorable outcome.

Action or event (something happens)	Your initial response	The result you're getting	How could you change your response to get a more desirable outcome?
Example #1: Your boss announces a change in staffing, and you no longer have any direct reports.	Complete shock: "How could he/she do this to me?" "What did I do to deserve this?"	You're angry, frustrated and feeling stressed about what this means for your future.	Exit the victim mode and ask yourself what role you played in this announcement. Were you doing your job effectively? Did your boss' perception conflict with your reality?

Example #2: A colleague resigns and you've been tasked with his/her workload until the new hire arrives.	You feel stressed and overwhelmed.	You doubt yourself; you're not sure you can handle this or even want to handle it.	You were tapped for a reason. You are a valued team member; decide what you need to succeed — more help, recognition, etc. How can you look at this situation to get a better outcome?

When You're Not Adaptable

Danger exists on both sides of the adaptability spectrum. Results are delayed or grind to a halt when you're too flexible *and* when you're too rigid. Indecisiveness, losing sight of your objective, being dumped on or getting paralyzed by the pursuit of unlimited possibilities are all products of too much flexibility.

If you are too rigid — in addition to potentially appearing difficult to work with and therefore less valuable to the organization — you cut yourself off from creativity and innovation. You also cut yourself off from the flow of work life and the give and take of the day, which can generate alienation, unnecessary stress, drama or panic. Rigidity is generated from two sources: an unwillingness to accept possibilities or an unwillingness to proactively contribute to the possibilities. Unbending characteristics of rigidity include:

- *The superiority complex:* "I know everything there is to know; there's nothing more to learn; I'm more experienced than everyone else; it's my way or the highway; my colleagues never have anything useful to add; they are never right."
- *The apathetic/inferiority complex:* "I can't handle all of these tasks; I like my comfort zone and don't want to rock the boat; I show up

79

and do the least possible to get by; I don't get paid enough to do more; let someone else take the lead; I'm not going to speak up, my suggestions are never considered anyway; what's the use of learning more, nothing is going to change around here; I won't get promoted; I've got my routine, leave me alone; I'm afraid of change; I am not creative, innovative or proactive."

Adaptability and Getting Ahead

To honor the role of adaptability in being your best and delivering your best work, your goal is to find the middle ground. Stand firm in your resolve to achieve your vision, but be willing to respond, bend and bounce back in the name of achieving better organizational results.

How well do you embrace both external (change initiated by someone else) and internal change (change you drive)? Examine your reactions to change. Even when change "happens to you," you can choose to allow the possibilities.

Below are strategies for strengthening your flexibility, resiliency and adaptability at work.

Embrace change as an opportunity for growth. When change occurs — change in your direct report, management team, job function or role or daily tasks — don't immediately think of it as a burden on your life and start the pity party, without first considering how the conditions could be conducive and beneficial to your growth. How could a benefit to the organization ultimately impact you? If you don't know, ask.

Peel back the layers of resistance. When you look at the many hats you wear every day on the job (problem solver, innovator, executer/doer, creator, team member, client contact, manager, leader, customer service representative), are there any roles or skills that bring up resistance, fear or hesitation? What is really behind those emotions? Are you really feeling uncertainty, isolation or de-valued?

Have you ever had a thought or actually said to a manager or teammate, "No, I'm not going to do that!" What was behind your answer — fear of an increased workload without true benefit to you? Uncertainty, feeling that you do not have the right skills? Plain old laziness? Notice your resistance and identify where you might be limiting yourself for advancement because you're not as adaptable as you could be. Remember, defensiveness creates resistance and suffering. Take a closer look to examine what's really behind your feelings.

Be open and inclusive as a way to generate the best result. Are you quick to shut others out because you know better? Think twice the next time you dismiss an idea or suggestion: it may be a strong support for an even better outcome. Adopt a growth mindset instead of a fixed one. Genuinely listen to other points of view to help you form more complex opinions of your own.

Keep a "can-do" attitude. One of my former bosses noted that one of the cruxes to a successful career in the company was a "can-do" attitude. Approach every task, situation and challenge with a resounding "Yes I can!" response, even if the butterflies of doubt flutter and you silently ask yourself how you'll be able to deliver. Something amazing happens when you say "Yes!" with excitement — your mind figures out a way to make it happen. And here's a helpful hint: visualize yourself succeeding and see the final outcome. The act of visualization creates a picture in your subconscious, which then creates a tension telling your brain, "Hey, I saw the picture, it can be done." Start to execute and follow any intuitive hunches about how to get it done; those are your subconscious mind trying to help you out. Turn to Chapter 11 for more information on visualizing.

Use discernment instead of judgment. Observe the possibilities, draw conclusions, come to consensus, make decisions and move forward. Discernment also means you're able to pick up every aspect of what is occurring without having to judge people and/or ideas — as in compare, diminish, make wrong or feel better than. People judge because they are threatened in some way. You can discern without judging and still have a strong point of view and opinion, be adaptable and add value.

Create a drama-free zone. Just as you can control your responses, you can control your environments and set them up to support you. Your workplace and your health/wellness are two important environments in your life (others include relationships, home life, financial, etc.). Raise your standards and decide to eliminate — or seriously limit — drama from your environment. Teach others how you want to be treated and set demands. Perhaps you need to stop acting as a sounding board for others, unless they also conclude to create solutions and take action. Stop listening to or participating in gossip — it's a waste of energy. Learn how to bounce back from setbacks with a "deal with it and move on" attitude. Feel what you need to feel, get it out, release it and move forward.

"Up level" your comfort zones. Everything you want to achieve in work and in life lies right outside your comfort zone. "Up level" is defined by stretching yourself and taking your current actions up a notch. Raise your standards to always strive for the best, learn and develop yourself.

Perception vs. reality. Does your perception of a situation match its reality? Beware of getting stuck inside your own little bubble at work. Make sure the perception you have about your work, your performance, your value and results matches those of your managers and teammates. Engage in honest dialogue, ask for and elicit honest feedback.

Experiment with the power of detachment. As much as you'd like to, you cannot control everything. Acceptance and surrender are keys to detachment. Whether it's a thought, feeling, emotion, ask yourself, "Can I let this go? Can I accept it as it is?" When you surrender and let go, you create space for something better. (See Chapter 3 for the discussion on detachment.)

The irony of easing stress lies in your ability to release control or the need to control. Our bodies naturally respond to stress and the emotions that it generates with a fight or flight syndrome: confront it head on or run. On my journey to thrive, I found that easing stress or anxiety (or any other feeling) is really about distancing yourself from the emotion. Hale Dwoskin of the Sedona Method encourages us that "We have emotions, but we are not our emotions." We have stress, but we are not stress. We have anxiety, but we are not anxiety. Simply put, as hard as you want to hold onto what you are feeling, you are not defined by what you are holding.

Try this exercise to demonstrate the point. Hold one hand out, palm facing the ceiling. Place a pen (or other small object) in your palm. Your palm represents you; the pen or object, your emotion. For our example, let's say your emotion is stress. Roll the object around in your palm. Notice, it's touching your hand, but it's not attached to you. Let the pen roll for a few seconds and think of how the stress is there, but it's not defining you. When you're ready to release the stress, just flip your hand over so your palm faces the floor. The pen, or stress, falls to the floor effortlessly. Take a moment to notice how that felt. Effortless? You can drop stress or any emotion just like you dropped the pen. All it takes is an awareness, space and the choice to detach from your emotion.

Now pick up the pen and return to reading!

Chapter Summary

✓ Adaptability is measured by how well you can adjust readily to changing conditions and environments. Your ability to embrace change, bend and bounce back while remaining focused on organizational goals are prized traits in the workplace. Adaptability means you do what it takes to generate the best results.

✓ Managing stressful situations begins by changing the way you respond to the situation. Stress is generated from fear: fear of the unknown, fear of not meeting a deadline, fear of not keeping a commitment, fear of _____(you can fill in the blank). Transform your energy by transforming your thoughts and emotions away from fear and anxiety to tranquility and calm.

✓ The most important factor in measuring your adaptability is examining how you respond to situations generated by an unpredictable workflow.

✓ What outcomes are you accepting at work that are less than desirable? Every outcome you are experiencing is the result of an action plus your reaction. How could you change your response to get a more favorable outcome?

✓ Additional strategies for improving your adaptability: embrace change as an opportunity for growth; address your resistance; be open and inclusive as a way to generate the best result; keep a "can-do" attitude; learn how to drop judgment and use discernment; create a drama-free zone and discover the power of detachment.

Take Action Challenge

How can I apply these principles to be more adaptable, flexible and resilient at work? List five actions you want to continue doing, stop doing or start doing.

1._____
2._____
3._____
4._____
5._____

Chapter Conclusion

In this chapter, you explored the role of adaptability in your pursuit for excellence. The next chapter provides 12 stress-busting strategies to help you remedy tough situations.

8

Tips to Thrive/Stress-Busting Strategies

"Stress comes from unkept agreements with yourself. You can relieve stress only by canceling the agreement, keeping the agreement or renegotiating it."
— *David Allen, Ready for Anything*

Ease stress and elicit a more even-keeled response in tense situations and you'll become a more productive, focused and happier worker. There's a direct correlation between your ability to manage yourself and influence others in pressure situations and producing quality results for everyone.

Here are 12 remedies to reduce stress.

1. Take a 3-minute respite from your day. Fill your belly with...a breath.

When you are stressed at work or have spent the last few hours zeroed in on a task, undoubtedly your breath is short, shallow and in the chest. Shallow breathing reduces the amount of energizing oxygen to the body and the brain and can leave you feeling physically and mentally drained. The solution? Take a belly breath. Sit up tall, feet flat on the floor, move your spine away from the back of the chair, hips toward the edge of the seat and breathe three deep, full breaths. On the inhale, let the breath fill your lower rib cage and the belly (not the chest). Imagine stretching the intercostal muscles between each rib bone like an accordion. Let the belly expand on the inhale and release on the exhale. Focus on your exhale and let the breath slowly leave the body. The act of slowing down and lengthening your exhales lowers cortisol levels in response to stress and increases endorphins and serotonin (mood enhancing neuropeptins.) You'll immediately feel calmer.

2. Generate tranquil thoughts.

When in doubt, repeat the serenity prayer.

God grant me the serenity to accept the things I cannot change;
the courage to change the things I can;
and the wisdom to know the difference.

3. Go outside.

Joyfully breathe in fresh air and reconnect with nature; a great reminder that you are one tiny part of a much larger and amazing universe.

4. Eliminate caffeine, other stimulants, refined sugar and processed foods from your diet.

Caffeine and sugar exacerbate cortisol levels and compromise the immune system. Instead choose more fruits, vegetables and whole grains and make sure you are hydrated. A good rule of thumb for your daily water intake is to drink half your weight in ounces.

5. Move your body.

Exercise increases circulation and energy and sends blood to the brain, improving your thinking. You don't need a 30-minute workout to feel the positive impacts: take the stairs or walk around the block. Send the blood flowing to other parts of your body with a couple of simple stretches.

6. Take a good multi-vitamin.

Stress uses up nutrients — including Vitamins C, B-Complex and magnesium, calcium, potassium, zinc and copper[18] — at an extremely high rate. You can quickly become semi-malnourished from even moderately high stress, so it is important to eat as well as you can to provide the most nutrients to your body.

7. Strengthen your support system.

Communicate with family and friends and ask for help. Most people who are able to cope well with stress have strong social support networks with family, friends and even pets.

8. Establish clear boundaries.

Make a commitment to yourself to establish clear boundaries that curtail their ability to take up your time, energy and emotional space. This means both outer boundaries, such as limits on the amount of contact you have with someone or avoidance of certain situations, and inner boundaries, such as switching your focus from negative thoughts about yourself and others to something useful or positive. Take every opportunity to bring into your life more of what makes you happy, gives you energy and helps you feel good. Don't be afraid to say "no" when someone asks you to do something. Learn your limits. You can't do it all and you shouldn't feel guilty about it.

9. Express your thoughts and feelings.

Open up. Speak your truth. Keeping the lid on your voice is stressful. Learn how to express your feelings appropriately by not insulting or hurting others. Place the focus on you, not them by stating, "I feel angry" instead of "You make me feel angry." This will help maintain and improve the important relationships in your life.

10. Smile.

The physical action changes how you feel inside, which changes how you behave and how your body reacts. In a recent study, subjects who made the physical action of smiling — even though it was just from holding a pencil in their mouths without any emotional content — reported feeling happier than those who didn't make this facial gesture under the same conditions.[19] Take the opportunity to smile more!

11. Get enough sleep.

Give your body a chance to recharge and heal, and your mind a few moments of silent solace each day so you are refreshed and ready to take effective action. Getting a good night's sleep is an essential part of reducing the effects of stress on your body. Your body does most of its healing, repairing and replenishing during sleep. You may be surprised at what a difference eight to nine hours of good quality, restful sleep a night can make to your health and sense of well-being. Know how many hours of sleep you need to perform at your best.

12. Practice time management.

When you're feeling overwhelmed with the amount of tasks on your to-do list, prioritize them according to their urgency (pressing timeline) and importance (task assigned by your boss, action needed to progress on a goal, self care etc.). Here's a strategy from time management guru Steven Covey[20] on how to prioritize your actions by importance and urgency. Create a grid with four squares on a blank piece of paper and organize by "urgent and important," "urgent but not important," "important but not urgent" and "not urgent and not important." Categorize your tasks accordingly.

Tackle the "urgent and important" first. Be mindful of how much time you spend on the second category, "urgent but not important." Be sure to make progress on the "not urgent but important" at some point during the week, even if you dedicate just five minutes. You'll feel lighter and more energized when you take action towards your goals. And work to remove the "not urgent, not important" items off of your plate entirely.

URGENT and **IMPORTANT**	URGENT but **not important**
These tasks include: Assignments from your boss or client; time-sensitive actions supporting your goals. Examples include: *Return client call this afternoon. Report due to boss on Friday. Kids' early school dismissal.*	These tasks include: Time-sensitive tasks that don't support your goals; actions to help colleagues; fire drills. Examples include: *Review colleague's report tonight. Tasks that are not urgent, but you procrastinate until the very last minute.*
IMPORTANT but **not urgent**	**not urgent and** **not important**
These tasks are usually the actions you need to take on your most important goals, but there's no time-sensitivity. Examples: *Exercise. Putting together healthy eating menu for the week or packing lunches. Meeting with your boss to discuss your career goals or having tough conversations with colleagues to set boundaries.*	The items in this category can be eye openers. Where are you being pulled off your game, or asked to spend your time in areas that don't support your core goals? Examples include: *Your "shoulds," "musts," "have-tos." They don't bring your joy or fulfillment. It's time to reexamine your commitment.*

Chapter Summary

✓ Ease stress and elicit a more even-keeled response in tense situations and you'll become a more productive, focused and happier worker. There's a direct correlation between your ability to manage yourself and influence others in pressure situations and producing quality results for everyone.

1. Take a 3-minute respite from your day. Fill your belly with…a breath.
2. Generate tranquil thoughts.
3. Get outside.
4. Eliminate caffeine, other stimulants, refined sugar and processed foods from your diet.
5. Move your body.

6. Take a good multi-vitamin.
7. Strengthen your support system.
8. Establish clear boundaries.
9. Express your thoughts and feelings.
10. Smile.
11. Get enough sleep.
12. Practice time management.

Take Action Challenge

How can you put any of these 12 strategies to work for you today? What's the action you will take and by what time today?

_____
_____
_____

Chapter Conclusion

You've now explored two Thrive 9 to 5® elements: energy and adaptability. In the next chapter, you will move onto the third element: focus.

9

Focus

Saturday, July 17 at 2 pm: I sat down to write this chapter and thought about what I wanted to say about focus. But ironically, all thoughts about concentration eluded me. I decided to review the outline for the remaining chapters one more time on the white board — snatching the dry erase marker and abandoning my keyboard. I spent a productive hour outlining, and moved on to something else.

Monday, July 19 at 2:40 pm: I sat down to write this chapter for the second time, but felt a gnawing headache coming on courtesy of the big sugar-laden iced tea I drank at lunch. Those 56 grams of sugar gave me an instant boost, but left me feeling very scattered soon after. (Full disclosure: yes, I am a work in progress and just chalked it up to experiential research to share with you!) Focus, focus, focus! I committed to finishing this chapter this week, so I just need to get grounded and start typing. Let me check my inbox one more time before I type…

Why is it when we want to accomplish something, we let distractions interfere and get the best of us? Why do we lose control and focus?

ADD? Lack of drive or motivation? Lack of energy? Soft boundaries? Or all of the above? Whether I'm in an office of 200, or working as a solopreneur in my home office, I still struggle with focus and concentration and so do my clients. There are always distractions!

Through my practice of yoga I have learned that our "monkey mind" generates self-induced distractions. You are familiar with the situation: the minute you sit down to focus, your mind starts wandering in 20 different directions… "I'm hungry, I'm thirsty, I wonder if any clients are trying to reach me, will my date from last night call me, what time is it, what am I going to do this evening, how is traffic, is it going to rain?" Yoga and meditation teachers encourage you to bring yourself back to stillness the instant you

91

notice you wandered. Because in the workplace you can't waste time wandering. You really need to tame that monkey pronto!

It takes four minutes to recover from a distraction — not including the time it takes to address the distraction. Simply put, if you stop what you do to check e-mail 15 times a day — you're wasting one full hour! Other external distractions include cell phone beeps, e-mail chimes and a Facebook wall beckoning your name, as well as the colleagues who barge in your cube with wild abandon for non-urgent chit chat.

Think of the last time you were completely absorbed in a task — writing, compiling a report, brainstorming, researching, making phone calls — and you lost all sense of time. How did you get started and remain in that state of focus? How did you control your mind and your environment, and what did you do to limit distractions? The key to concentration and getting absorbed in your work is to replicate that environment so you can easily slip back into your ideal focus zone.

Being in your zone is intricately connected to being in the flow and generating a greater level of happiness and fulfillment. In his seminal work *"Flow: The Psychology of Optimal Experience,"* Mihaly Csíkszentmihályi (known as the "Father of Positive Psychology") outlines his theory that people are most happy when they are in a state of flow — a state of concentration or complete absorption with the activity at hand and the situation. Csíkszentmihályi describes flow as a completely focused motivation where you are "being completely involved in an activity for its own sake. The ego falls away. Time flies. Every action, movement and thought follows inevitably from the previous one, like playing jazz. Your whole being is involved, and you're using your skills to the utmost."[21]

The zone is that place of high energy, focus and enthusiasm where we sail along performing at our best. A point guard driving the lane in the championship game with two seconds left on the clock and a two point deficit, a sales team wrapping up a stellar presentation that would double the size of their profit unit and a prosecuting attorney addressing the jury in the heat of a courtroom trial — we all have seen others shine in the zone. And we have all experienced the zone ourselves. You know you're in the zone when you're excited and enthused to be tackling a project, so focused and absorbed you lose track of time. Or when you rock a presentation or client call or juggle a dozen tasks and mark them complete one by one at the end of a productive Monday.

In this section, you'll define what it takes to get in your zone, so you can turn it on and turn it off like the flip of a productivity switch. The hallmarks of being in your thrive zone are feelings of being at your best mixed with spontaneous joy, even rapture. To be caught in any other emotion will block you from the zone. Your zone is a single-minded immersion and represents perhaps the ultimate in harnessing the emotions in the service of performing and learning. In flow, the emotions are not just contained and channeled, but positive, energized and aligned with the task at hand.

Your Ideal Focus Zone

1. **Know your zone.** When was the last time you were in your zone, totally engaged in an activity that you lost track of time? What were you doing and what did it feel like? Describe the scene as best you can. What was it about the environment, your mood or the situation that allowed you to be totally absorbed in the activity? How can you apply that experience the next time you need to get in the zone and focus?

   _____
   _____
   _____
   _____
   _____
   _____

2. **Get clear.** What does "focus" look like for you right now and what do you want it to look like? Why is being focused important to you? What does it (or will it) cost you if you don't make a change? State your answer in terms of dollars if you can.

   _____
   _____
   _____

_____
_____
_____

3. **Pinpoint your distractions**. What needs to be done to eliminate or limit them?

_____
_____
_____
_____
_____
_____

4. **Determine the length of time that you can stay focused on one task before being distracted.** This becomes a critical factor in your time management strategies. When you know how long you can stay focused, you can begin to schedule your day around these intervals and allow yourself appropriate time to get things done, eliminating stress and/or the need to rush. You can also put in place breaks to stretch or rewards to motivate you. For example, "I'll get up for a snack in 30 minutes or once this page is complete, whichever comes first." Not sure of the length of your focus zone? Time yourself the next time you engage in a task and see how long you can get absorbed without distraction.

_____
_____
_____
_____

5. **Stop tolerating the intolerable and improve your focus.** Let's face it, we tolerate a lot and it takes our eye off of our game. And complaining, whining, shaming or blaming does nothing to eliminate the daily irritations. When you feel you have to tolerate something or someone, it implies the situation is less than desirable. Telling yourself it's OK to settle for less drastically lowers your self-esteem and your inner drive to be healthy. These

hindering influences tire you out, squash your natural creativity and allow you to accept mediocrity. It's time to get rid of these irritations!

The benefits of being toleration-free and clearing the past include freeing up time and energy for a higher quality of life. You will feel lighter as you stop trying to manage situations that drain your energy. List five things you are tolerating at work or in your personal life and the action steps you're going take to eliminate them.

What is irritating me?	How can I fix it?	Who can I delegate all or part of it to?	By when?

6. **Describe your ideal *focus zone*.** What do you need to start doing, continue doing or stop doing to create your ideal focus zone?

Environment: What do you need to clean up in your environment to set your ideal focus zone? Clear your schedule, clear your space, limit disruptions (people, technology) and detach from your incessant e-mail-checking habits. Phone off — check. E-mail silent — check. Door closed — check.

_____

_____

_____

_____

Mental: How will you control your monkey mind? What do you need to do to get yourself centered and clear your head for the task ahead? How will you eliminate your excuses or rationalizations for not being focused? What is keeping you from moving forward?

_____
_____
_____
_____

Motivation: What is going to motivate you to stay focused? A reward? The payoff from achieving a goal? State your motivation and purpose. Give yourself 60 minutes to complete a task and start a countdown clock. Keeping the visual in your face allows you to get serious!

_____
_____
_____
_____

Physical, nutrition, and hydration: What do you need to eat or drink to generate the level of intensity and determination you desire? Remember, sugar and processed foods can make you scattered. Make sure you're getting your nutrients, protein and fiber for long-lasting energy. Small doses of caffeine also add to mental alertness.

_____
_____
_____
_____

Your standards: Make a declaration that you're going to control your ADD, limit distractions and eliminate multi-tasking. Where can you improve your habits and environment to be working in full integrity? Personally, it infuriates me when I'm talking on the phone with someone who is multi-tasking. Their actions are telling me that they found something more important to do, but they don't mind wasting my time. Therefore, I raised my standards to never multi-task on phone conversations and devote my full attention to the person or persons on the other end.

_____

_____

_____

_____

Chapter Summary

✓ Distractions abound everywhere. Whether they are self-induced or brought on by others and your environment; you have the choice to create boundaries to limit all of them.

✓ Remember, it takes four minutes to recover from a distraction — not including the time it takes to address the distraction.

✓ Think of the last time you were completely absorbed in a task — writing, compiling a report, brainstorming, researching, making phone calls — and you lost all sense of time. How did you get started and remain in that state of focus? How did you control your mind and your environment, and what did you do to limit distractions? The key to concentration and getting absorbed in your work is to replicate that environment so you can easily slip back into your ideal focus zone.

✓ Being in your zone means a state of concentration or complete absorption with the activity at hand and the situation. The zone is that place of high energy, focus and enthusiasm where we sail along performing at our best. Know what it takes to get in your zone, so you can turn it on and turn it off like the flip of a productivity switch.

Take Action Challenge

What are five actions you need to take (or stop doing) in order to create your focus zone?

1. _____

2. _____

3. _____

4. _____

5. _____

Chapter Conclusion

You've now explored three Thrive 9 to 5® elements: energy, adaptability and focus. In the next chapter, you will move onto the fourth element: purpose.

10

Purpose

"Purpose provides activation energy for living." — *Psychologist Mihaly Csikszentmihalyi, author of Flow: The Psychology of Optimal Experience*

We live in a nation of high achievers and define ourselves by the work we do. We identify ourselves by our rank, title, salary and bonus packages. Yet climbing higher and earning more money are not the only factors contributing to our happiness at work. Studies conducted by the Gallup Organization, Towers Watson and other employee engagement experts point to additional factors driving fulfillment, including having the opportunity to do your best and positively impact the organization's products and services, as well as personal alignment with the company's mission/purpose.

Your roadmap to thrive is lined with the desire for personal achievement matched by the need to contribute to the greater good and be valued as a part of something larger than yourself. Human performance expert Dr. James P. Brennan says, "Our deeper sense of purpose can function like an internal navigation system, using our own unique compass points…to guide us through all kinds of outer conditions." Master the coordinates of your personal GPS — a strong sense of who you are, what you do, where you are going and why — to catapult your confidence and engagement on the job, and ultimately create an internal drive strong enough to keep you steady and withstand external pressures and distractions.

Define the coordinates that contribute to peak performance for yourself — those that define your contribution to the larger organization (your purpose), and those that drive personal achievement (your vision and goals).

But first, a few clarifying definitions. *Purpose* defines who you are, what you do and the value that you bring to the organization's bottom line. Your *vision* is your ideal picture of what you want for your future. And your *goals* are the measurable objectives or milestones to achieve that vision. Clearly defining all three will fuel desire and motivation for better health, happiness and fulfillment. In fact, after interviewing hundreds of global giants in business, athletics, government and the nonprofit sectors for his book *The Success Principles*, author Jack Canfield concluded that one of the differentiating factors among high achievers is their unusual clarity about their purpose, vision and goals.

Let's examine each concept separately. This chapter will focus on purpose; the next chapter, vision and goals.

Purpose

Undoubtedly you arrived on your first day of work armed with a job description, training and instructions on what's expected of you. But how many of us show up for work every day knowing our true purpose? As employees or entrepreneurs, we may know our organization's purpose, mission, vision and goals, but have we clearly defined our own purpose as it aligns with the larger organization? And how often do we get lost in the "doing" or "achieving" and forget who we are? Purpose is one of the motivating factors driving your results.

Clearly articulating your purpose and how your role is aligned to support the organization's core goals catapults your confidence and your ability to deliver and exceed expectations. When you are clear about who you are and the value you bring, you're better able to prioritize and execute tasks, and measure your effectiveness and success. Your core purpose and values become your guiding principles, which remain fixed in the face of changing business responsibilities, roles and practices. It gives you a strong foundation to have the mental, emotion and physical energy to show up every day ready to do your best work. And the result is greater fulfillment and happiness at work.

Here is an example of how getting clear on her purpose helped an accomplished professional eliminate unnecessary drama at work and keep laser-focused and energized through a tough transition.

My client Jill was at a crossroads. A high-energy go-getter leading a team of 15 account managers and product developers, she was bumping up against countless rejections and an endless myriad of office politics in pursuit of advancing her team's agenda. The frustration left her listless at the end of each day. She started to see her team's energy and enthusiasm waning, and their results, creativity and work ethic started to suffer. At the same time, she was being considered for another job within the company, but needed to handle the situation carefully in order to maintain her stellar reputation and keep her team's drive and momentum strong. And the other opportunity wasn't yet a sure thing.

One of the first steps we took was redefining her purpose. Instead of wallowing in the frustrations of doors closing in her face and ditching her team for the lure of something better, we zeroed in on the value she delivered to the organization and what she needed to feel fulfilled at work. Instead of defining herself by the roadblocks she encountered that made her feel like a failure, we took a step back to look at the bigger picture. Her value to the organization was serving as a dynamic leader who brought the best out in her staff and who continually delivered quality products and service. She crafted a purpose statement and began repeating it to herself daily. It read: *I am a high-energy leader who uses my enthusiasm and tenacity to inspire and empower my team and serve my clients.* Jill's purpose statement zeroed in on her true value; the exact elements that lit her up inside.

What's Your Purpose @ Work?

In simple terms, your Purpose @ Work is who you are and the value you deliver. It is more than a job description. It's an inspiring, one to two sentence depiction of what you stand for and your core values. Think of it as merging you (your strengths, interests, passions) with your value to the organization (your core job function and expectations.) A strong purpose statement will help you stay motivated and focused, even during times of transition or when doors shut in your face.

Here are examples of other purpose statements:
- *I use my drive and organizational skills to revolutionize the way my clients measure their success.*
- *I am a strong woman who empowers others to work in integrity and achieve their potential.*

- *I am a powerful executive, leading from my heart and standing in my greatness.*
- *I am an inspiring manager always exploring infinite possibilities.*
- *I am calm confidence connecting purpose and power for the greater good.*

Now it's your turn. To help you craft your purpose statement, follow these steps[22] and clearly define your Purpose @ Work.

1. List one or two adjectives that describe you as a person. At your core, who are you? If you were to ask your boss, direct reports, colleagues, friends or family, what adjectives do they (or would they) use to describe you?

2. List two of your unique personal qualities, such as enthusiasm, creativity, problem-solving abilities or skills that you bring to the job. Pick the personal qualities that you most enjoy expressing and that you feel best differentiate you. When your work life is ideal, who are you? (See Appendix A for examples.)

3. Define how you express those qualities at work. List the action verbs that describe how you put those qualities into practice. When your work life is ideal, what are you doing at work? (See Appendix B for examples.)

4. Combine 1–3 above into a single statement. My Purpose @ Work:

_____

_____

_____

_____

_____

Take Action Challenge: Put Your Purpose Statement to Work

Post your purpose statement at your desk. Keep it visible and repeat it often. Use it as a daily reminder and motivator. See yourself working in your integrity, delivering value and being fulfilled.

Find purpose in everything you do. Wandering along a path without a purpose can induce feelings of disillusionment and isolation and throw a wrench in your ability to feel fulfilled on the job. If at anytime you doubt what you're doing or how it applies to the larger vision of the organization, ask for clarification. A task that isn't inherently interesting can become more meaningful and more engaging if it's part of a larger purpose.

Take note when you feel disillusioned or disconnected from your colleagues or the larger organization. Describe your feelings and identify what is behind them. Are you being valued? What do you need to ask for and whom do you need to ask? How do you want or need to be valued?

_____
_____
_____

Take ownership and responsibility for your tasks and role. Living and working in integrity means taking responsibility for all that occurs in your life and on the job. I'm not talking about playing the role of a martyr and assuming the blame for situations, but rather asking yourself what role you played in the situation. Take ownership and proactively seek to find the solutions or necessary adjustments to avoid the problem in the future. In order to handle and resolve situations, you must also drop your complaining, shaming and blaming.

If you were to take 5 percent more responsibility for your success at work, what would that look like? What would you do (or be doing) differently? How do you limit yourself?

_____

_____

_____

_____

_____

Chapter Conclusion

You've now explored all four Thrive 9 to 5® elements: energy, adaptability, focus and purpose. In the next section, you will get clear on what you want and how to put your intentions into action. Part IV will address:

1. Clarity of your vision and goals. Decide what you want. You must be crystal clear on where you want to go and how it will feel once you're there. Set specific and measurable goals.
2. Ability to clear the path. You must remove all the obstacles, which means getting others out of your way and getting out of your own way.
3. Plan of action. Create a daily success routine that keeps you in your zone.

When you have these three simple factors defined and lined up on your behalf, nothing can stop you. Sure you'll have moments of weakness and doubt, you may even cave in. But you can always pick yourself back up and start again. A strong inner drive allows you to redefine success as making progress in the direction you want to go and enjoying the journey each step of the way. Let's move forward by clarifying where you want to go with your vision and goals.

Part IV

The Thrive 9 to 5® Action Plan

11

Your Vision & Goals: Decide What You Want

"When you are clear, what you want will show up in your life, and only to the extent that you are clear." — *Janet Bray Attwood, co-author of The Passion Test: The Effortless Path to Discovering Your Life Purpose.*

In order to ignite your strong internal drive, you must get clear on what you want to achieve and envision it as if it's already here. That means not only deciding on the outcome, but also the details of what it looks and feels like. Then act as if you already have it.

Your vision becomes your guiding light: a positive, affirmative picture that generates momentum and motivates you to take consistent action. Creating a clear image of your desired result empowers its achievement because clarity empowers you to act. Zoom out or reframe the situation in order to gain a broader perspective of what you really want. This will help you recover from any incident where you may falter, hit the snooze button or indulge in the cake. Small slip-ups are not that debilitating once they are reframed against a grander picture. Envisioning the picture of a healthy, vibrant you helps ease any obsessive nature and resistance to progress, while shifting the focus to feeling good instead of agonizing over past failures.

Creating a vivid picture also ignites your subconscious mind. Once your subconscious sees a vivid picture, it starts to work towards achieving that picture as if it is reality. According to Robert Fritz, an expert on the creative process, the discrepancy between what you have and what you want creates a powerful dynamic in the process of creation, called "structural tension." A basic tenant of nature states that tension seeks resolution. Think of putting a single rubber band around your current reality and stretching it to meet your new vision. Your reality gets pulled in the direction of your new vision.

This tension generates energy that is used in the process of bringing your vision to reality. By envisioning what you want, your subconscious mind will go to work. You may come up with new ideas or generate possibilities you haven't thought of before. The phone may ring and someone offers you a solution, or you find the resource you need exactly at the right place and time. Set your vision and watch closely as the impossible becomes probable and the probable becomes reality. Just remember, there are no coincidences! You create your results with your thoughts and images, so what you think and picture makes a difference.

You can repeat the process and create a compelling vision for all areas of your life: career/business, financial, relationships, health and personal development.

Give yourself permission to think bigger and grander — beyond the incremental measurements of weight, clothing size or daily caloric intake. Look inside yourself. What does healthy and vibrant feel like to you? What are the qualities you want to experience all day and night? What improvements do you want to make to your health and wellness? It's time to get real and get specific. Your vision for your health and wellness is uniquely yours. Make sure it works for you and is not a "could," "should," "would," "must" or "have to" imposed by someone else. Take a hard look at what you want and re-ignite a passion for a healthier, happier future.

This is your chance to redefine your own success. Imagine feeling energized and vibrant and living at a healthy weight. What if you had more focus and could produce more quality work in less time? How would your life change? What would success look like?

Imagine optimal health coming to you easily and effortlessly. You don't have to be obsessed about food, calories, pounds or inches or kill yourself to get there. The Thrive 9 to 5® program is designed to help you make incremental changes in your mindset and workstyle that will last a lifetime. This isn't about fads or strict diet regimes. It's about common sense and tuning into your own body and brain.

Imagine you have the time. Your health and the energy take priority. Without them, everything else at work and in life suffers. Imagine that you drop the pain and suffering. Achieving your vision is not hard work. You create your own suffering, and therefore, you can eliminate your own suffering, too. Healthy living is an effortless expression of who you are.

Define Your Vision

What is your ultimate vision for your career? What is your ultimate vision for your health and wellness? What kind of life do you want? Think back to your inventory on energy, purpose, focus and adaptability in Chapter 2. What are some of the habits you would like to adopt in your routine? What is it that you ultimately want to achieve and how will you when you are successful? Beyond achievements, describe your ideal work environment. What are you doing, how are you putting your skills to use? What are you experiencing? How are you valued? What types of people (energy, personalities, characteristics) are you surrounded by?

Here is an example of a clear vision for health and career:

I am a healthy and vibrant woman and I take care of my physical, emotional and mental well-being. I arrive each day at work ready to take on the day; I eat well and fuel my body to sustain my energy. I avoid the foods, behaviors, conversations and thoughts that drain me. I take time to prepare healthy meals and always choose the best foods possible. My immune system is strong and supports me. When times get stressful, I know how to re-center myself and remain level-headed throughout the day. My physical strength empowers me. I have a daily success routine that starts with a moment of silence in the morning and ends with a recap of my day.

Now it's your turn. Take a few moments and close your eyes to visualize your ideal work life and answer the questions above. Write down what you see, feel or hear. (Log onto www.thrive9to5.com/vision.php for an audio clip walking you through this exercise).

My vision for my ideal work life:_____

_____

_____

_____

_____

_____

_____

One of the most powerful actions you can take on the path to achieving success is writing down your vision. The second most powerful action is sharing your goal with someone else and verbally declaring your intentions. Write them down and share them with a loved one, friend or colleague.

And remember your mindset. Notice the first response that pops into your mind when you read your vision. Are you energized, excited, pumped up? Do you believe you can do it? Or are you sighing at yourself with a snide remark? "Yeah right, that will never happen." Or "I've got such a long way to go." Whatever thought popped into your mind: you are right, 100 percent correct. And you will continue to be as long as the thoughts arise. Notice where you still have doubts and return to your Inner Advertiser[SM] affirmations in Chapter 3 to drown out the negative.

Commit to Action: Set Measurable Goals

"The clearer you become about what you truly love and desire, the stronger your conscious intention becomes, and this helps the rest of your brain respond in an organized way." — Dr. Andrew Newberg and Mark Waldman, authors of Why We Believe What We Believe

Once you have your vision, you need to create the roadmap to fulfill it. Ignite your strong internal drive by setting measurable markers or milestones to track your success. State the goals you'd like to achieve will take you closer to your vision. Here are a few pointers to remember when setting S.M.A.R.T. [23] goals:

- Be **S**pecific: What are you going to do? Why is your goal important at this time? And how are you going to do it?

- Make it **M**easurable: Define your goal in a way that you can measure success. How will you know you achieved the goal and what does success look like? For example, instead of declaring a goal to "eat healthy," make it more precise — "to eat a serving of vegetables at every meal," or "to swap out my afternoon junk-food snack with a piece of fruit."

- **A**ttainable: Is your goal within your reach and do you really want to do it? Make it yours. Don't fall into the trap of being pressured by others to achieve certain goals. Your mother may have told you to lose some weight, but is this something you want for yourself, or are you just going to hear her voice echoing in your head? Drop the "shoulds," "musts" and "have tos." You don't have to do anything you don't want to do; and it will only create more resistance. You can only adopt a healthy lifestyle without a struggle when the goal is yours and yours alone. There is nothing more powerful than saying this is what I want to do and moving forward with wild abandon. There's no energy or time wasted when you work in alignment with your true desires.

- **R**ealistic: While anyone can achieve anything, make sure you believe you can achieve your stated goal. If you know it's impossible to cut out sugar from your diet completely, start with eliminating it one day a week, then progress from there. Set yourself up for success and allow yourself to feel good about your progress.

- **T**ime-bound: State what you want to achieve and by when. Set an exact date and time for your deadline. For example, set a goal of working out for 20 minutes 3 days this week by Friday at 5 pm. At 5 pm on Friday you can measure whether or not you've achieved your goal.

Here are some more examples of how to take your original statements and craft more specific and measurable goals:

Statements	_Specific and Measurable Goals_
I want to lose weight.	I want to feel healthy and alive at 155 pounds by March 1 at midnight.
I need to eat healthier.	I consume at least one serving of vegetables every lunch and dinner during the next 30 days.

I should go to the gym.

I find 30 minutes twice a week to use the treadmill, walk or lift weights during the next two weeks.

I want to de-stress.

This week, I will identify what triggers my stress and experiment with trying to respond instead of react to stressful situations.

Your Health and Wellness Goals

List three doable, measurable goals that you would like to achieve during the next 12 months for your health and wellness.

1. _____

2. _____

3. _____

Once you define your goals, answer the following questions:

How will your life/career be better? What's the value to you?
_____
_____

If you don't change, what is the cost to you?
_____
_____

What are the action steps you must take to reach those goals? What do you need to continue doing, stop doing or start doing?

Action Steps for Health Goal 1:

_____
_____
_____

Action Steps for Health Goal 2:

_____
_____
_____

Action Steps for Health Goal 3:

_____
_____
_____

Your Career Goals

List three doable, measurable goals that you would like to achieve during the next one, three and five years for your career.

1-year goals:

_____
_____
_____

3-year goals:

_____
_____
_____

5-year goals:

_____
_____
_____

Once you define your goals, answer the following questions:

How will your life/career be better?

_____

_____

If you don't change, what is the cost to you?

_____

_____

What are the action steps you must take to reach those goals? What do you need to continue doing, stop doing or start doing?

Action steps for 1-year career goals:

_____

_____

_____

Action steps for 3-year career goals:

_____

_____

_____

Action Steps for 5-year career goals:

_____

_____

_____

Chapter Summary

✓ In order to ignite your strong internal drive, you must get clear on what you want to achieve and envision it as if it's already here. Your vision becomes your guiding light: a positive, affirmative picture that generates momentum and motivates you to take consistent action. Creating a clear image of your desired result empowers its achievement because clarity empowers you to act and also ignites your subconscious mind. Once your subconscious sees a vivid picture, it starts to work towards achieving that picture as if it is reality.

✓ By envisioning what you want, your subconscious mind will go to work. You may come up with new ideas or generate possibilities you haven't thought of before. The phone may ring and someone offers you a solution, or you find the resource you need exactly at the right place and time. Set your vision and watch closely as the impossible becomes probable and the probable becomes reality. Just remember, there are no coincidences! You create your results with your thoughts and images, so what you think and picture makes a difference.

✓ What is your ultimate vision for your career? What is your ultimate vision for your health and wellness? What kind of life do you want?

✓ Set goals which will be the milestones along the way to achieve your vision. Follow the SMART structure, so your goals are:
  o **S**pecific
  o **M**easurable
  o **A**ttainable
  o **R**ealistic
  o **T**ime-bound

Drop Obsessive Thinking

Losing a certain number of pounds or reaching ideal digits on the scale are markers for success along your journey, but shouldn't become an obsessive focus. If you know this is a problem for you, then rephrase your goal. Instead of "I need to lose 15 pounds," say "I'm feeling healthy and alive at my ideal weight." Pursuit of a specific number — whether it's a pant size or daily calorie count — elicits feelings of deprivation, lack, pain and suffering. Also, release the hold on any obsessive goals that you've had for 10+ years — for example, the goal of fitting into the skinny jeans that have been sitting on your closet shelf for the past decade. How many times have you beat yourself up when you stepped on the scale and didn't reach the magic number or felt like a failure when you couldn't zip up your skinny jeans? Obsessive health fanatics rarely succeed over the long term and quite frankly aren't fun people to be around. Balance between achieving and allowing is key.

Take Action Challenge

What's one action you can take today, in the next hour, to get you closer to your health or career goal? Instead of waiting for the perfect time, get to work and do it now!

What's the action you will take and by what time today?

_____

_____

Chapter Conclusion

You've completed the first step to your action plan: getting clear on exactly what you want and how you plan to get there. The next chapter will help you pull together all of the action items you've identified from your work so far.

12

Your Thrive 9 to 5® Action Plan
Get Into Your Thrive Zone!

"That first step you take is the longest stride." — *"If Today Was Your Last Day," Nickelback*

You began this journey to improve your health and wellness at work and learn how to operate at peak performance. In the previous chapters, you've generated a keen awareness for what's working and not working for you in your daily routine and you've identified the core components of your Thrive 9 to 5® Mindset and Workstyle. You defined your purpose and vision, identified your energizers and energy drains and assessed your focus and adaptability. You uncovered elements of your mindset and workstyle that no longer serve you. You have identified new standards of living and working, started thinking in new ways and committed to halting the deadly routine that has you stuck in a rut. Now it's time to dump the bad habits to make room for healthier behaviors and create your own thrive routine.

Shoot For the Moon Not Mediocrity

You know your career success depends on how healthy you are, how well you fuel yourself and how well you can engage your body and mind in peak performance. Make a commitment to yourself that you'll never compromise your health and happiness at work for anything. It doesn't mean that you're compromising your work ethic. It means that you are aware of what you are doing to your body and mind day in and day out and you commit to taking care of it so you can function at optimal levels. Commit to being your best, so you can be sharper, smarter, quicker, more innovative and creative at work, not to mention more effective and productive.

It's time to put yourself first. When you feel better, happier and fulfilled, everything else in your life flows better. You're more efficient, focused and able to get more done. You feel more engaged in what you're doing. The peace of mind and balance you derive from healthy thoughts also helps you rest, unwind easier and sleep sounder. Achieve a high level of attunement and you will know when you can push it and when you need to rest, both personally and professionally. Your thrive routine becomes a trusted guide to living your life. It's not about sacrificing health or happiness for success; it's about optimizing your performance for all three.

The Thrive 9 to 5® program guides the development of your plan to achieve your best results at work and at home; earn more money and career advancement; create more time for life's priorities and strengthen your personal/professional relationships. You now have the strategies and tools to summon and direct the energy, adaptability, focus and purpose you need (when you need them) to live and work at your best. Jump back in the driver's seat of life, start making healthy habits stick and achieve peak performance.

Throughout my journey to thrive, I learned and invented techniques and rituals to help me stay focused and put all of my "to-dos" into action. This chapter includes some of the gems that worked for me and for my clients. Start with motivation.

Know What Motivates You

Motivation is the impetus to take action. We are all motivated in different ways. According to Dave McClelland's "learned needs theory," humans are driven to act by one of three factors:

- *Achievement:* You are motivated by getting things done, taking responsibility and risks, setting goals and performance standards.
- *Affiliation:* You are motivated by approval from others; you seek relation to others to share challenges, take action and celebrate successes.
- *Power:* You are motivated by the desire to control or influence events and people.

No one factor is more effective than the other, it's just a matter of generating awareness for what resonates with you. If achievement motivates you, you need a clear plan that includes your vision, goals, action steps, timeline and tasks that you can check off as you complete them. This chapter directs you to a free online tracking grid to help you measure success. Pick a reward for each goal: How will you celebrate once you achieved them: special purchase, trip or self-care action?

If affiliation motivates you, choose an accountability partner (colleague or friend) who can take this journey with you. Commit to partnering, share your goals and timeline. Check in with each other once or twice a week to report on your progress, your challenges and the action items you commit to for the week. An accountability partner will help hold your feet to the fire and provide companionship for added motivation.

If you are motivated by power, take a hard look at your environments and know what you need others to be doing to support you. What needs to change and who can help change it? Where can you ask for support? Where can you influence your environment? And what does success look like? Be clear and concise.

The bottom line is know what you need in place — the actions you need to take, your environment, support system — that will motivate you to take consistent action and make long-lasting behavior change.

Create the Space for Change

Our bad habits stem from living and working in a state of unconsciousness. Clearing the fog demands a pause in the action to create a keen sense of awareness.

When you are stuck or caught in a bad routine, you operate in unconscious habit mode. You go through your day oblivious to what you are feeling, oblivious of your actions, until you hit crisis mode (such as blowing up at a colleague or fainting from not eating enough nutrients). It feels as though external forces run your life; you are not in control. Someone else is at the helm of your ship, and you fall merciless to the rocking and rolling of the waves and wind and can only react to what is happening.

When you create more space in your life, you create a pause, long enough for you to slow down, wake up and make conscious decisions.

Space is room to pause after a stressful interaction, instead of a knee-jerk reaction.

Space is taking your time while eating. Do you scarf your lunch or snacks down at your desk, multi-tasking? Tune in to the barbaric nature of your actions. Eating consciously also helps improve your digestion.

Space is creating a delay before you give in to temptation. Drink a glass of water before you race to the vending machine for a cola.

Space means taking time to rest. If you've gone through a hellish week at work (or two in a row), working long hours well into the evenings, make sure you block off time to rest and recuperate. That means saying no to social functions, errands that can wait and projects around the house that aren't urgent. And if you're antsy sitting around doing nothing, learn how to find ease in restlessness.

Space is accepting the fact that sometimes you just need to be — be still, be quiet, be alone — without a to-do list or being constantly in motion. Give yourself permission to live fully in the moment without your mind lingering somewhere planning the future or reliving the past. It's a foreign feeling, I know. For those of us who were comfortable in the unconscious zone, this truly is a detoxification. Your mind and body are so used to racing from one thing to the next, or tackling five actions at one time, it feels strange to have nothing planned or nothing to do. You immediately want to fill that void with something.

Stop every once in a while to check in, "Am I in unconscious mode or am I fully here in the present? How can I create more space in my life? Where can I stop or slow down and be fully present?" You will be amazed at the answers that pop into your mind when you slow down to listen to them.

Get to the Source

Think about the habit you are trying to break. Write down when this habit began and identify the events leading up to it happening. Determine what is reinforcing the habit. Then decide how you are going to address it. Ask yourself why you revert back to or hang on to this habit. What need is it filling and how can you get that need met elsewhere or with a healthier habit?

Your Thrive 9 to 5® Action Plan: Putting Your Mindset and Workstyle to Work for You!

The Thrive 9 to 5® approach is about making incremental changes. I'm not asking you to re-haul your entire routine and life. In my experience as a coach, total life makeovers work when you're up against the wall: receiving a medical diagnosis or hitting rock bottom. Total re-hauls take a do-or-die mentality and a huge level of personal discipline and motivation. If you've got it, go for it.

For the rest of us, chunking down big changes into manageable pieces eases the journey and makes the road more palatable. We all know that life happens, especially when you're working in a demanding environment. Slow and steady with persistence wins the race.

Start with a focus. What's most important to you at this time? What are the most pressing changes you want to make? You get to define your action plan. This is your chance to take back control of your work life and craft the daily success habits that will boost your energy and keep you healthy, happy and fulfilled at work and in life. You are in the best place mentally and emotionally and whatever you decide is going to be the best decision for you now. Trust and go with it.

Build your 90-day thrive routine by prioritizing the mindset and workstyle elements you've uncovered in this book so far. Identify the top 10 priority action steps and habits that you want to take to maximize your health, happiness and success at work. You will commit to following these habits every day for 30 days. At the end of the month, you can re-evaluate and revise for the next 30 days.

You'll repeat this twice. Remember, it takes 30 days to break on old habit and 90 days to change your behavior for good.

Here are the elements to your plan:

Get clear on what you want. Review your health and wellness and career goals. Pick two health and wellness goals and your one-year career goal as targets to work towards in the next 90 days. If they are large goals that cannot be achieved in the next three months, that's O.K. Keep your goals as stated and commit to working towards them. Progress beats out procrastination every day.

What do you want to achieve and by when?

#1) Health Goal:_____

#2) Health Goal:_____

#3) 1-Year Career Goal:_____

List your insights and commitments from your Thrive 9 to 5® Mindset and Workstyle. Let's review all of the notes you made to yourself during this journey about the actions you need to start doing, continue doing or stop doing. List them all and we'll prioritize them in the next exercise. In the case of actions you need to stop doing or ask others to stop doing around you (setting stronger boundaries), state the action you will take to make that happen (remember, you cannot control someone else's actions).

Chapter 2, page 23: List any action items from your inventory.

_____
_____
_____
_____
_____

Chapter 3, page 44: List what actions you want to take to raise your standards and set better boundaries.

_____
_____
_____
_____
_____

Chapter 5, page 58: List your actions.

_____
_____
_____
_____
_____

Chapter 6, page 75: List any energizing tips you'd like to adopt.

_____
_____
_____
_____
_____

Chapter 7, page 84: List any action items to improve your adaptability and flexibility.

_____
_____
_____
_____
_____

Chapter 9, page 98: List any action items to improve your focus.

_____
_____
_____
_____
_____

Chapter 12: Your Thrive 9 to 5® Action Plan

Chapter 11, page 112-113: List your action steps from your goals.

_____
_____
_____
_____
_____
_____
_____
_____
_____
_____

Choose your top 10 new thrive habits. From this list of actions and habits above, what are the top 10 mindset or workstyle items that will help you achieve your three goals or move closer to achieving them? Review the action steps above and list those that you *want* to take in the next 30 days, not actions those that you think you "should" or "have to" take. You want to set yourself up for success, not create drudgery or added stress. Ask yourself, "Do I really want to do this, and will it leave me feeling energized and alive or lethargic and irritable?"

If you've listed more than 10 actions, here's an easy way to decide which ones take priority. Read the first and second lines above and ask yourself which is more important to you and which gets you closer to your vision for your career and health. Then compare that answer to line three…and that answer to line four…and that answer to line five and so on. Move through the tasks from each chapter. Circle the line that rises to the top of your list, and then repeat this process until you have 10 circled. List your 10 habits below.

What do you want to experience? Your thinking? Feelings? Behaviors? What old habits will you stop and what new habits will you start? Where do you want to be in 90 days?

123

My top 10 thrive habits and action items:

1. _____

2. _____

3. _____

4. _____

5. _____

6. _____

7. _____

8. _____

9. _____

10. _____

Your Thrive 9 to 5® Daily Routine

Follow your 10 habits daily for 30 days. Keep your list handy and use the weekly chart available from the web site (www.thrive9to5.com/actionplan.php). Work these 10 habits into your day and notice how you feel. Is it easy or are you struggling? Give yourself permission to take the time you need to work these 10 success habits into your day. You don't need to do it perfectly. Drop perfectionism and eliminate the need to beat yourself up when you slip. Try again tomorrow. Keep moving forward no matter how many setbacks you have. Remember, progress beats procrastination every day.

Create a daily ritual, set intentions and visualize. You are doing something great for yourself — your body, mind and career. You have the choice of looking at this list like any other to-do list that may generate feelings of anxiety, doubt or plain old misery. Or you can look at it as an opportunity to create every day (and the month and entire 90 day period) exactly how you want to see it unfold.

In order to create your day, you set an intention in the morning (or night before) visualizing yourself going through your day. Beyond executing tasks, think about the energy you want to generate, the feelings you want to feel and the interactions you want to experience. As discussed in Chapter 11, the power of visualization is undeniable. Every single thought you have is a statement of your desires. You are a product of all the thoughts you have thought, feelings you have felt and actions you have taken up until now. And the thoughts you think today will determine your experiences tomorrow.

Experiment with the morning routine below and see how your day unfolds!

1. Take a few minutes to breathe deeply, get quiet and settle your mind.
2. Review your vision, goals and purpose statement. Close your eyes and daydream for a few minutes. See yourself achieving the goals, notice what it looks like, the images and emotions. Feel what it would be like to achieve those goals.
3. Set your intentions for the day and visualize how you want it to unfold. What would you like to see happen today? What level of energy do you want to generate and maintain? Where do you need to focus or be flexible? How are you going to show up? Pick one theme as your intention for the day.
4. Go about your day and watch what unfolds!

Unleash your Inner Advertiser^{SM} with affirmations. Keep the positive statements from Chapter 3 visible. Repeating affirmations daily helps you rewire your mind, stay positive and align your thoughts and beliefs with the healthy actions and results you desire. Post your goals and affirmations on sticky notes on your computer, note cards on your mirror or framed reminders on your desk, use them as motivators for action.

Daily review. At the end of each day, track your progress on your daily habits and note how well you did on your intention(s). What went well and what could you have done better? Are there any new energizers or drains that you are aware of?

30-Day check in. After 30 days straight, evaluate your progress. Don't judge or punish yourself, just take an honest assessment. What's working and why? What's not working and why not? What do you need to adjust in your daily routine for the next 30 days. Readjust and move forward.

Reward yourself. At the 90-day marker, take pride in all that you achieved and celebrate! Keep an attitude of gratitude and appreciate every step along the way, no matter how small.

Conclusion

"Come to the edge."
"We can't. We're afraid."
"Come to the edge."
"We can't. We will fall!"
"Come to the edge."
And they came.
And he pushed them.
And they flew.
— By Guillaume Apollinaire

Congratulations and thank you for taking the journey! Whether you picked up this book to break a bad habit, reduce stress in your demanding work environment or achieve peak performance, I am grateful for your dedication and commitment to being the best you.

It is my intention to help you thriving — from 9 to 5 — or whatever hours you keep. Whether thrive means pushing to a new comfort zone, snapping out of unconscious living or getting crystal clear on what kind of life you want to live, let the strategies and techniques in this book serve as a guide, motivator and reminder that you can do it!

Sometimes it takes a gentle nudge or a push off the proverbial cliff to convince yourself that you can have it all, everything you desire...all the success, achievement, balance, fulfillment and vibrant health that you want. Take the first step. Take one step each day for the next 90 days...and soar!

I want to hear about your 90-day journey and your successes. Please feel free to e-mail me at Kristi@thrive9to5.com and let me now how you're thriving!

Sources

[1] Pink, Daniel. *Drive: The Surprising Truth About What Motivates Us.* New York: Riverhead Books, 2009.

[2] William Glasser Institute, The Glasser Approach/Choice Theory: www.wglasser.com.

[3] MacPhee, Robert. *Manifesting for Non-Gurus: How to Quickly & Easily Attract Lasting Results.* Encinitas, CA: HeartSet, Inc., 2010. (Pages 16-18)

[4] Weber, Ellen, Ph.D. "The Brain on Music." Brain Leaders and Learners: Practical Tactics from Neuro Discoveries with Dr. Ellen Weber. November 14, 2008. http://www.brainleadersandlearners.com/multiple-intelligences/musical/the-brain-on-music. (I discovered the technique of pairing recorded affirmations with classical music tracks from Ann Webb's "Ideal Life Vision" www.ideallifevision.com; and from John Assaraf's "Brain Training System," www.johnassaraf.com.)

[5] For more information on The Sedona Method® visit www.sedona.com. For more information on The Work by Byron Katie® visit www.thework.com. For more information on EFT® visit www.eftuniverse.com.

[6] Christie, Catherine. "Food and Mood Relationships:" http://www.faqs.org/nutrition/Met-Obe/Mood-Food-Relationships.html

[7] Protein content for foods listed in chart are found at www.nutritiondata.com. Shaklee Cinch® bar nutrition information found at www.shaklee.com. Stonyfield Farm® yogurt nutrition information found at www.stonyfield.com. California walnuts nutrition information located at www.walnuts.org.

[8] Fiber content for 8-ounce glass of extra pulp orange juice found at www.tropicana.com.

[9] Fiber content for fruit located at www.nutritiondata.com.

[10] Mayo Clinic Staff, "Caffeine: How much is too much?" Nutrition and healthy eating: http://www.mayoclinic.com/health/caffeine/NU00600

[11] Sleep Research Center. "Nutrition Report: A high sugar content, low caffeine drink does not alleviate sleepiness but may worsen it." *Women's Health Magazine,* December 2006. (Page 22).

[12] Dohadwala, Mustali M.; Hamburg, Naomi M.; Holbrook, Monika; Kim, Brian H. et al. "Effects of Concord Grape Juice on Ambulatory Blood Pressure in Prehypertension and Stage 1 Hypertension." *American Journal of Clinical Nutrition* (2010 92: 1052-1059; doi: 10.3945/ajcn.2010.29905).

[13] Junger, Alejandro. *Clean: The Revolutionary Program to Restore the Body's Natural Ability to Heal Itself.* New York: HarperOne, 2009. Recipe adapted from menu on http://goop.com/newsletter/15/.

[14] Ibid.

[15] Krieger, Ellie. *The Food You Crave.* Newtown, CT: Taunton Press, 2008. (Page 61).

[16] Wansink, Brian, Ph.D. *Mindless Eating: Why We Eat More Than We Think.* New York: Bantam Books, 2006.

[17] Canfield, Jack. *The Success Principles: How to Get From Where You Are to Where You Want to Be.* New York: Collins, 2005. (Formula adapted from E=R+O, Page 3.)

[18] Wellness Councils of America. "The Low Stress Diet: Eating for a Healthy Immune System in a Stressful World." (2006) www.welcoa.org/presentations/files/_.../low_stress_diet_handouts.pdf

[19] Munger, Dave. "Just Smile, You'll Feel Better." *Cognitive Daily.* Nov. 27, 2007.http://scienceblogs.com/cognitivedaily/2007/11/just_smile_youll_feel_better_w.php.

[20] Covey, Steven. *The 7 Habits of Highly Effective People.* New York: Free Press, 1989, 2004. (Page 151).

[21] Geirland, John. "Go with the Flow: According to Mihaly Csikszentmihalyi, great web sites are not about navigating content, but staging experience." *Wired Magazine,* 2004. http://www.wired.com/wired/archive/4.09/czik_pr.html

[22] Adapted from The Canfield Training Group's life purpose exercise, 2007.

[23] Doran, George T. "There's a S.M.A.R.T. way to write management's goals and objectives." *Management Review,* November 1981, Volume 70 Issue 11.

Appendix

Appendix A:
Qualities That Describe You *(for the exercise in Chapter 10)*

Read through the list quickly and circle 10 words that best resonate with you. Go with your first instinct, don't ponder it too long. Read through your circled words and choose your top two.

Abundance	Connection	Expert	Leader
Accomplish	Content	Facilitator	Learning
Acquire	Contributor	Family	Loving
Adventure	Controlling	Foster	Magnificence
Alert	Courageous	Freedom	Mastery
Articulate	Creator	Fun	Move Forward
Artistic	Daring	Glamour	Nurturing
Assemble	Dedicated	Glow	Observing
Assisting	Delightful	Govern	Open-minded
Athletic	Dependable	Grace	Orchestrating
Attaining	Designer	Grant	Original
Attentive	Detective	Grateful	Passionate
Attractive	Director	Guide	Patient
Augmenting	Discern	Healthy	Peaceful
Awe-inspiring	Discover	Honest	Perceiving
Be present	Distinguish	Honoring	Perfect
Be the best	Dreamer	Humor	Persevering
Beautiful	Educator	Imagination	Persuading
Bliss	Elegance	Impactful	Planning
Brave	Emote	Improving	Playful
Building	Emphasize	In touch	Predominate
Calm	Encourage	Influencer	Preparing
Capable	Energizing	Informing	Prevailing
Catalyst	Enjoying	Ingenuity	Providing
Coach	Enlighten	Inquisitive	Quest
Comforting	Enrolling	Inspiring	Radiance
Compassionate	Entertaining	Instruct	Refined
Committed	Excellence	Integrating	Reigning
Community	Exhilaration	Integrity	Relating
Complete	Experience	Inventing	Religious
Congruent	Experiment	Laugh	Respond

Responsible	Set standards	Synthesizing	Uncover
Risk-taking	Sincere	Tasteful	Understanding
Ruling	Spark	Teaching	Unique
Satisfied	Speculate	Thoughtful	Uplifting
Security	Spiritual	Thrill	Venture
Seeing	Spontaneous	Transforming	Vulnerable
Seeking	Stimulating	Triumph	Wealth
Sensing	Strengthen	Trustworthy	Winning
Serenity	Superior	Truth	Writer
Serving	Supporting	Turn	

Appendix B: How You Express Those Qualities

Read through the list quickly and circle 10 words that best resonate with you. Read through your circled words and choose your top two. *For the exercise in Chapter 10.*

Account for	Budget	Create	Drive
Act	Build	Critique	Edify
Adapt	Calculate	Cure	Edit
Address	Care	Dance	Educate
Administrate	Change	Debate	Empower
Advertise	Classify	Decorate	Encourage
Advocate	Climb	Decide	Enforce
Align	Collaborate	Define	Enlist
Allocate	Collect	Demonstrate	Evaluate
Analyze	Communicate	Deliver	Examine
Anticipate	Compare	Design	Exercise
Appraise	Compile	Detail	Expedite
Arrange	Compose	Detect	Experiment
Assemble	Conduct	Develop	Explain
Assess	Consult	Diagnose	Express
Assign	Contribute	Direct	Facilitate
Assimilate	Control	Discover	Fix
Assist	Cooking	Dissect	Forecast
Balance	Coordinate	Draft	Fundraise
Bargain	Counsel	Draw	Gather

Graph	Modify	Reconcile	Study
Guide	Motivate	Record	Style
Identify	Navigate	Recruit	Summarize
Influence	Negotiate	Reduce	Supervise
Initiate	Nurse	Reflect	Support
Innovate	Observe	Relate	Systematize
Inspire	Operate	Repair	Think
Install	Organize	Report	Train
Interpret	Perform	Reproduce	Transform
Invent	Persevere	Research	Translate
Implement	Persuade	Restore	Understand
Know	Plan	Review	Utilize
Lead	Prepare	Risk	Update
Learn	Prioritize	Schedule	Trouble-
Lecture	Process	Sell	Shooting
Listen	Program	Serve	Unify
Lobby	Promote	Shape	Validate
Model	Publish	Simplify	Visualize
Manage	Reason	Speak	Win
Map	Recommend	Stage	
Mediate		Stimulate	

Acknowledgments

Thank you to my mom and dad, Kathy and Rich Daniels, for your unconditional love, support, occasional kick in the pants and for always believing in me, even on the days when I doubted myself.

Thank you to my sister Becky and brother-in-law James for your love, support and for hosting me for months on end at your West Coast haven and mecca of sun, sea and fun...and oh yeah...writing!

Big hugs to Ian and Avery, the greatest little entertainers and my best excuse for a writing break. Your smiles, giggles and screams light up my heart. Auntie K loves you!

To the entire McFadden and Daniels clan — Lin, Frankie, Dana, Ed, Debi, Mark, Sandee, Doug, Katie, Eric, Ian, Lauren, Emily, Joe, Gwen, Todd, Ashley, Shawn, Lexie, Rickie, Charlotte, Gram, Jim and Rella — for your love, support and belief in me. And also for the occasional, "Are you done with that book yet?!" In memory of Mary, Jean, John and Vince for instilling the "I can do anything" mantra in our lives. Special thanks to Ann DeRenzis for giving me my first set of speaking opportunities back in P'burg, and to Maryann McFadden for being an inspiration and role model for persistence, keeping the faith and living your dream!

To Amina Makhdoom, you are an exuberant ray of sunshine! It means the world to me to have a best friend who manifests like wildfire, inspires me every day to live my best life and dream a little bigger. I love you girl...you ROCK!

Thank you to Robin Fisher Roffer for being an inspiring light and mentor and for living your authenticity. Thank you to Jim and Camille Brennan for your guidance, support and precious words of wisdom.

Thank you to Danielle Bradley, Anita Sanchez, Kathleen Seeley, Dahlia Fakuda, Deb Farrell and Miro Fitkova for your friendship and for reviewing my manuscript. Your feedback, razor sharp minds and encouragement provided tremendous value to the final product! Special thanks to Holly Jones for your design counsel; to Joe Preston for igniting my entrepreneurial spirit and for always reminding me how smart I am; and to my Fairlington neighbor and fellow yogini, Christine Chirichella, for your friendship and editing prowess. Namaste!

To my amazing mastermind sisters: Tiffany Walke Peterson and Catey Gibson. Thank you for creating a safe space for laughs, tears, tantrums and being real. And for helping me to get crystal clear, holding me accountable and igniting my internal motivation to keep moving onward and upward. Ladies, you are fabulous!

To Terry Newhard, Shari Geller, Kay Reiss, Dawn Marie Kondas, Allison Conley, Georjean Trinkle, Patrick Grogan, Maritza Baakman, Tom Fitzgerald, Ken Knipmeyer and the entire NORWESCAP Board and family, for welcoming me to your team. My life as a solopreneur started off lonely in a small town, and I relished the opportunity to be affiliated with a team of enthusiastic, values-driven and fun individuals who manage to juggle 1,000 tasks at once while thriving with high energy and big smiles!

To Jack Canfield and everyone in his inaugural Train the Trainer class. I'm so grateful our paths crossed and I'm pumped up to know you're out there illuminating lives all across the globe. Shine on!

To the Lafayette College Skillman Library and Merrill Creek Reservoir communities: thank you for offering peaceful sanctuaries and breathtaking views to write this book. Thank you to the friendly staff at Panera Bread in Phillipsburg, NJ for supplying bottomless cups of comforting decaf and to the Shaklee Corporation for delivering my protein shakes and Vitalizers each month to keep my body energized, healthy and vibrant along this journey. Special thanks to the North Park community in San Diego and Claire de Lune coffee house for the upbeat tunes and smiles during the final month of editing.

About the Author

Kristi Daniels is a workplace performance coach with 15 years experience in mobilizing employees to take action and improving workplace productivity. A former senior vice president for a global consulting firm, she works with organizations and individuals turning lackluster sales and apathetic attitudes into driving forces for unprecendented growth. Her Thrive 9 to 5® program is a one-size-fits-you solution for working professionals to achieve peak performance and live at their best.

For more information on the Thrive 9 to 5® coaching programs, workshops and products for individuals and teams, please visit www.thrive9to5.com. To book Kristi to speak at your next conference or event, contact her at kristi@thrive9to5.com.

LaVergne, TN USA
20 December 2010
209594LV00003B/1/P